Disqualified?

What the Bible Says about Divorce, Remarriage, and Ministry

(Revised)

Disqualified?

What the Bible Says about Divorce, Remarriage, and Ministry

(Revised)

Dave Miller

SBC VOICES PUBLISHING

Sioux City, Iowa

Copyright © 2021 Dave Miller
Revised 2021
All rights reserved.
ISBN-13: 979-8742333463

v

DEDICATION

To Jenni, who has been with me for over four decades, for better and for worse, for richer and mostly for poorer, in sickness and in health, allowing me to write a book like this without defending or justifying my experience. As we get closer to the "till death do us part" I am thankful for your partnership in ministry.

ACKNOWLEDGMENTS

Thank you to Dr. Harold Hoehner, my favorite professor, though he never knew me! He assigned me this paper so many years ago and started my inquiry into this topic.
Thank you to the readers of SBC Voices who interacted, argued, and honed the ideas presented here.
Thank you to the many men (and a few women) who have contacted me about their desire to serve God and their sorrow and frustration about having been prevented from doing so by circumstances they regret and churches that refused to see past them. It is your pain that helped me to realize that this book needed to go to print, despite how some will receive it.

Contents

Preface

"Well, pastor, I just want to stick with what the Bible says."

My deacons and I were discussing whether to allow men who had been divorced to be part of the deacon ministry. To these good, godly, Bible-loving men the scriptural revelation was clear beyond dispute. Divorce eliminated a man from service as a pastor (elder) or deacon regardless of the circumstances, based on 1 Timothy 3 and Titus 1. Any other view was biblical compromise. These men were not trying to be difficult or belligerent, they were being faithful to their convictions. Our church is blessed to be led by men with spiritual backbone, who have the courage to follow their convictions.

We had a small problem that day, though. These faithful men's pastor (and the author of this book) did not share their convictions. My convictions, based on extensive study of God's word, lead me in a very different direction. I left that meeting that night with a task before me. My friends were convinced that the view I held had no biblical merit. I wanted to show them that while their commitment to truth was noble their view of the biblical revelation on divorce, remarriage, and ministry was not biblically accurate. I had a month, until the next meeting, to accomplish my task.

I began by digging into my files. Back in my seminary days I had done a research paper that surveyed the key biblical passages on divorce and then dealt primarily with 1 Corinthians 7 exegetically. I expanded on that research and by the time the next deacons' meeting rolled around, I overwhelmed the assembly with a fifty-one-page paper, eliciting wry comments comparing the length of my paper to the average length of my sermons. That paper later became a series of blogposts at SBC Voices which have remained active as the years passed. That paper, and the blogposts that follow, formed the basis of this book.

In the paper, in the blogposts, and in this book, I will argue as I did to my deacons, that the assumption that many have made through the years is not supported in Scripture. My good friend who made the statement I began with, who is now in heaven, was convinced beyond doubt that the Bible could only be interpreted one way. All divorce is sin and eliminates the divorcee from service as a pastor or deacon. My goal was to show him that the biblical evidence might not support his assumptions, that the evidence might not be so cut and dried, and that it might be possible to have a completely different view and still be faithful to God's word. That is my conviction. It is also my sad belief that the traditional view has led to unnecessary hurt and pain in the lives of people.

Even more importantly, I believe there is a gospel issue at stake here. When we fail to understand how grace works, how Christ cleanses and restores, how he rebuilds lives that have been broken by sin, even by divorce, we fail to understand and communicate the gospel clearly. This is no small issue. Of course, it is an issue that resonates with pastors and deacons and others who have suffered through divorce – for whatever reasons. It is an issue for all of us, even for people like me who married at age 20 and have been married to the same woman for over forty years. We must understand and apply the implications of the saving, cleansing, and restoring work of Christ to real-life situations like divorce, remarriage, and ministry. This book is an attempt to do just that. I had to try to convince these men that what the Bible taught on this topic was not what they had always assumed that it taught.

My dear friend went to his grave believing that his way was right – even my fifty-one-page paper didn't convince him. Often, our positions are so entrenched that we do not release them easily. But what I did that evening at our deacons meeting was at least get some of our more dogmatic men to admit that there was another way of looking at the biblical evidence and that their pastor's views were not based on compromise or cultural accommodation, but on a serious study of God's revelation.

In this book, I will present my findings to you. My request is simply that you consider the evidence. I am not naïve enough to believe that everyone who reads this will agree with me, but I would ask for a fair hearing. The stakes are high. In your church and mine are people whose lives have been chewed up by the failure of marriages. It is crucial that our ministry to them be biblical and in line with the message of the gospel – nothing less.

This is no easy task. The gospel is about both righteousness and sin. We cannot abandon the clear biblical teaching of the sanctity of marriage or ignore God's intent that a man and woman who covenant in marriage stay in that marriage for life. However, the gospel is about forgiveness and restoration as well. We cannot be gospel people if we fall off on either side – if we ignore God's righteousness or if we ignore his redeeming and restoring grace. As we approach these topics, we must look at the panoply of revelation on the topic to see the nuanced, deep, and full truth about divorce, remarriage, and ministry.

It is my prayer that this book will help you think through these issues deeply, carefully, biblically, and prayerfully.

What the Bible Says about Divorce, Remarriage, and Ministry

Preparing the Project: An Overview

Gathering the Tools and Preparing for the Task Ahead

All Scripture is inspired by God and is profitable for teaching, for rebuking, for correcting, for training in righteousness, so that the man of God may be complete, equipped for every good work. 2 Timothy 3:16-17

Chapter 1: Preparing the Project

Once, the evangelical church sang in unison on issues related to divorce. Divorce was a sin – every time, regardless of the circumstances. Those who were divorced were not allowed in leadership roles in churches that took the Bible seriously. They were not pastors or elders. They were not deacons. In fact, in many churches they were marginalized and shunned socially, treated as second-class citizens of the kingdom of God.

That was easier to do in the "good old days." Divorce was rare; respectable people tended to stay in their marriages, even if they were miserable. On the street where I grew up there was one of "those" women. She had been divorced and even had a child out of wedlock. There was plenty of sin and dysfunction behind the other doors on Elder Lane, but those doors were closed and her sin were out in public for all to see. In those days, she was the rare bird, the odd ball on the clean streets of our Midwestern town.

Then, a (not so) funny thing happened. Divorce became commonplace in America and suddenly our neighborhoods and our churches were filled with people like "that" woman – in one generation her lifestyle went from rarity to norm. Isolating and ostracizing the divorced was no longer a viable option in this new world.

This whirlwind cultural shift was followed by an all-too-common pragmatic shift in the theology of the church. Our doctrines tend to change to reflect the culture in which we live. American Christianity has embraced a man-centered, therapeutic focus for our faith; the push for holy living has been swallowed up by the quest for happy living and the glory of God has given way to the good of man. Our highest pursuit is no longer the glory of God, but the good of the men and women who attend our churches. If standards must be altered, lowered or even abandoned entirely in this pursuit of happiness then so be it. The culture of the church has quickly adapted to reflect the changing culture of society.

The wife of the pastor of one of the largest churches in my community left him and they divorced. The pastor, from all I was told, was guilty of no adultery or infidelity, but the fact that he stayed in his pulpit for a couple of years after the divorce took place was evidence of a dramatic shift in attitudes. When I was growing up, he would have been out of his pulpit the day his wife left him. It is a new world.

Now there are divorcees on almost every pew, people who have been married several times, mixed families, "yours, mine and ours," – it is not the 50s anymore. This radical shift has found its way into the leadership of many churches. It is not rare to find divorcees among the leadership of many churches. As denominations struggle with issues like ordaining homosexuals, whether a man has been divorced seems to pale in comparison.

This tendency to mold our doctrine and practice to our culture instead of to Scripture has a long and unfortunate history in American

Christianity. The greatest moral stain in American history is the subjugation of Africans into slavery and the dehumanization of people made in God's image. Racism, discrimination and segregation were often not only tolerated but promoted within the church of Jesus Christ. During the slavery years, pulpits all over the South proclaimed that slavery was both divinely ordained and approved. We wonder how men could have read their Bibles and not seen the wickedness of such things, and yet we are doing the same thing today. Some read the Bible and justify a form of patriarchy that allows for the suppression and abuse of women in ways that would have offended our Savior who called for servant leadership and who always treated women with respect. At the same time, so-called evangelical feminists are performing feats of hermeneutical gymnastics so astounding that they defy logic and turn the Bible's teachings on its head. When feminism became the dominant thought of the day, suddenly they discover that 2000 years of understanding of the teachings of the Word on the roles of men and women were all mistaken. As homosexuality has become accepted (no, not accepted, but celebrated) in our world, suddenly many are suddenly "discovering" that those scriptures that seem to be prohibitions against homosexuality aren't really that at all. We missed it again. That is our sad tendency – what culture approves we discover in Scripture. When slavery was popular, we proclaimed it. When extreme patriarchy was the accepted norm, that was our doctrine. When feminism arose in America, suddenly egalitarianism was discovered in the Scriptures. As homosexuality gained acceptance in culture, some discovered new interpretations of the Bible that gave acceptance to it. Instead of being prophetic and calling sinners to repentance, we tend to seek the approval of our culture by molding our interpretations to the world around us.

This has happened in the church's views on divorce. When our culture placed a high value on lifelong marriage and looked askance at divorce, the church was right there to proclaim that marriage was meant to be "till death do us part." When cultural values changed, and marital fidelity gave way to the ethic of personal happiness, the church "discovered" that the Bible was about self-esteem and personal happiness. Church as group therapy replaced prophetic truth.

Our human solution to such cultural shifts is often wrong. "We need to go back to the old ways!" often means a return to the nostalgic past, not biblical ways. Our old ways often were no more biblical that the new ways are. The solution is to study the Scriptures and to find our views informed by them. The old culturally conditioned teachings were no more biblical than the new culturally conditioned ones are. Evangelical feminists abuse scripture to proclaim egalitarianism, but old-fashioned patriarchy was also a corruption of God's intent and the teachings of the Word. The modern trend towards approval of the practice of homosexuality is a perversion of the Bible, but so is the more traditional practice of disdain, ridicule, cruelty, and brutality. Often, both the traditional view and the modern view are equally unbiblical. Our goal must be to become biblical, not just to return to what is old-fashioned or traditional.

As we approach the study of divorce, remarriage, and ministry, we must remember this. The traditional view of absolute prohibition – that divorce is always a sin, that the divorced must never remarry, and that they are forever prohibited from leadership positions in ministry – is based on a misunderstanding of biblical evidence and of the implications of the gospel work of Jesus Christ. The more recent view that regards divorce and remarriage as insignificant ignores biblical principles of righteousness and holiness and also fails to understand the implications of the work of Christ among us.

Let us lay aside our preconceptions and dig into the treasures of God's word to observe its rich and nuanced teachings. Our first loyalty must be to God and his word. If what the Bible says offends either our traditions or our culture, we must be faithful to the word. Everything must be put under the piercing light of Scripture – our personal interpretations, denominational traditions, and ecclesiological practices.

Of course, we all believe that a fair reading of Scriptures will lead people to adopt our view on issues like this. The reader will have to search the Scriptures and judge whether I am able to make my case. My thesis is simple. I believe that the church has been guilty of constructing its view of divorce, remarriage, and ministry on the basis of tradition and cultural conditioning more than on actual evidence in the Bible. The traditional view goes beyond the Bible's teachings and ignores the thrust of the gospel, which is forgiveness, renewal and restoration. Others have abandoned scriptural teachings to adopt a no-fault, standard-free, position that is equally unbiblical. There are twin dangers to be avoided. We must not ignore the teachings of the word of God because they are difficult or offend our culture and we must not add to them based on our traditions and presuppositions.

That is my thesis and I hope to demonstrate that it is supported by an accurate rendering of the Bible's teachings. My hope is that the reader will agree.

In This Study

In this study, after a review of some preliminary concerns, we will survey the significant passages in the Bible that deal with the subject of divorce, looking for answers to several questions. Is divorce always a sin? Can a divorced person remarry? What positions of service can a divorced person hold in the church?

We will maintain that the truth lies neither with the traditional prohibitionist view nor with modern therapeutic views. The Bible teaches both the permanency of marriage and the fact that in a broken world there are exceptions that must be made. In such exceptions, remarriage is allowed. The gospel is about redemption and renewal and that demands that even serious and sinful mistakes of the past can be overcome by the power of God, that character can be rebuilt and the ability to lead restored.

We must maintain perspective. This is not a battle between those who love God's Word and those who do not. Those who hold to the traditional view do so because they believe that is what the Bible teaches. I disagree strongly with that view and think it is based on a faulty foundation, but in no way do I question their devotion to God's Word. Even those who allow their views to be shaped by culture often do so without ill intent. Some may have abandoned the Bible's teachings, but most are motivated by the love of Christ and the desire to help people. We can disagree, even strongly, with certain viewpoints without calling into question the motives or spiritual integrity of those with whom we disagree.

Do I believe that the traditional view fails to take into account the implications of the gospel of Jesus Christ? Yes! But do I believe that those who hold the view disdain the gospel? Of course not. None of us is perfect in our application of truth. Do I believe that some have compromised biblical truth to gain approval of people? Yes, I do. Do I believe that this comes from a heart of disregard for God and in word? In many, perhaps most, cases it does not. It comes from a failure to understand God's word, but not a failure to believe it. So, my hope and goal is that I could argue my point forcefully – that what I believe is both biblical and in line with the implications of the gospel in a way that other views are not. But I do so in full awareness and with the acknowledgement that those who disagree with me also love Jesus, love the word of God, and proclaim the biblical gospel. This is not a fundamental issue.

In fact, the church I serve as pastor operates with an unwritten policy that is different than my position. I have advocated my position, explaining what I believe and why I believe it. My position has been heard with respect, but there is still a large group who remain unconvinced. Since election of deacons (and pastors) requires a super-majority according to our bylaws, anyone with a history of divorce is not nominated to serve. I think the church misses out on some fine servants of God who could serve as deacons, but for the sake of unity and out of respect for those who disagree, we have made the choices we have made. I continue to serve my church joyfully. Of course, I wish everyone agreed with me and I will continue to advocate my understanding of the word. But until then, in spite of our disagreements on this issue, I can maintain full fellowship and gospel partnership with those with whom I disagree.

Defining the Views

There are nearly as many positions on divorce as there are teachers on the subject. Categorization of views necessitates simplification, perhaps oversimplification. Evangelical views are more of a continuum than fixed viewpoints, but we can form generalized categories while also recognizing almost infinite variations. The two major views stand on the ends of the continuum while other views lie between them. The view defined in this book is between the two positions and attempts to respect each while also showing their weaknesses. We are, of course, seeking to examine views held within the Evangelical community, by those who hold to the Gospel and to the authority of the Word of God.

The Prohibitionist View

On one end of the continuum lies the prohibitionist view. The prohibitionist, who believes strongly that he is upholding biblical values and standards, generally holds immutably to three propositions. First, it is always a sin, contrary to God's will, to seek a divorce. Second, those who have been divorced, whether they are the "guilty party" or no, are prohibited by Scripture from remarrying. Such remarrying they say, is an act of adultery with Jesus condemned. Finally, they believe that those who have been divorced or are married to those who are divorced are prohibited from every serving in the biblically defined leadership positions of pastor, elder or deacon.

There are variations among prohibitionists. Some allow that divorce is permissible when adultery is present, but still prohibit remarriage and deny that restoration to leadership in the church is possible. Some distinguish between divorce prior to conversion and divorce as a Christian. It is not a monolithic stance. What unites prohibitionists is opposition to those who have been divorced and remarried being restored to leadership positions in the church. They tend to see themselves as the defenders of biblical standards, of the sanctity of marriage, and as opponent of moral decay.

Proponents of this view uniformly have a high view of Scripture and a willingness to stand for what they believe the Bible says, even if it is contrary to what is popular in culture. Their refusal to compromise on the issue, while sometimes frustrating to those who hold other views, is noble and convictional, evidence of commitment to the word of God. For the same reasons, proponents can be frustrating, believing that other views are based on compromise rather than exegesis and prizing their traditions as biblical mandates.

If the traditional prohibitionist interpretation concerning divorce, remarriage, and ministry is not biblically accurate, it is hurtful to the church of Christ. If they are upholding biblical principles, then their uncompromising conviction is a blessing. If they are rigidly applying traditions not based on Scripture, they are forcing an unbiblical standard on the people of God, then the position is dangerous and hurtful. People who are biblically qualified for service, who could be a great blessing to the church, are being excluded from positions of service. Unbiblical condemnation is often being poured out on those who have already repented and are being renewed by God. If it is not biblical, then the prohibitionist position is destructive the Body of Christ.

That leaves a simple question. Does the Bible advance the prohibitionist view? If it does, we should hold to it with courage. But if it is not biblical, we should abandon it with haste.

The "Compassionate" View

At the other end of the spectrum from the prohibitionist view is the "compassionate" view. Divorce is traumatic – it rips apart homes and families, devastates lives and brings heartache to all. Ever heard a celebrity assert that even though he or she was getting a divorce that the couple would remain "best of friends" as they moved forward. Of course, reality never really matches that fiction. Divorce sweeps through a family and leaves a swath of destruction in its wake. Where there is brokenness, the church must minister. The church's duty is to minister the healing of Christ where sin has brought brokenness. Every believer agrees with that.

The compassionate view uses brokenness as a justification to withhold standards. Why would we "punish" people who have already been hurt so badly? When we adopt a therapeutic model of ministry, our goal is to make people happy, healthy, and whole. The church's role is to help people through life's hard times and to fix their broken lives and we should focus on bringing joy, help and healing. We should comfort, not judge. The therapeutic church loses sight of God's holiness and focuses more on people's self-esteem. Pleasing God by righteous actions can give way to helping people feel better about themselves and find healing and happiness in their daily lives.

When a divorce comes, then, the concern is less on upholding biblical standards for marriage or maintaining the holiness of the church, but on helping the hurting to find comfort, peace and healing. Of course, it is right to minister to the hurting and to help those whose marriages are crumbling to find hope in Christ, but it is wrong to assume that ignoring biblical standards is the path to happiness. When we assume that health and healing come by making people feel better about themselves instead of bringing them into a right relationship with God through repentance and obedience, we have failed in every way. This does not please God and it does not heal people who were made to walk in obedient relationships with the Father. Therapeutic religion that ignores repentance and holiness is false hope and ineffective.

This view could also be called the "permissive" view, because it adopts a permissive attitude toward sin and toward the violation of God's Word. Proponents are willing to compromise God's Word to help people feel better about themselves and find happiness. As simply as it can be put – in this permissive view, compassion trumps truth.

Those who hold to the compassionate/permissive view give precisely the opposite answers to the three questions we asked earlier of the prohibitionists. Is it a sin to divorce? Not if your marriage is making you unhappy. May divorced people remarry? Of course, if they cannot find happiness in the single life God would want them to find someone who will meet their needs and bring joy to their hearts. Can divorcees serve in leadership roles in the church? Of course. We cannot exclude them and make them feel unwanted.

There is merit to this view. Its adherents care about people and their pain, as should every believer. Jesus grieved over sin's effects on people's lives. Christians can sometimes, in our uncompromising proclamation of truth, become harsh and unkind to those who are struggling with sin and its effects. People going through the trauma of divorce do need compassion. They need to be welcomed into the church, provided fellowship and sympathy and a warm environment in which to heal. Too often, the church has made divorcees feel unwelcome in the fellowship of the church, as if they were second-class members.

We do not show compassion, however, when we compromise truth. Doctors do not help us when they ignore the symptoms of disease and give us painkillers or other drugs to make us feel better. We want our doctors to tell us the truth and deal with the problem. When we see the brokenness of sin, we must diagnose it and deal with it truthfully. Divorce is a symptom of sin and it should be dealt with at its roots as God intended if we want healing.

There was an infuriating cable show called Intervention. Each episode focused on an addict who was ruining his or her life with drugs or alcohol. There was always a family member who was helping to keep the addict under slavery to their addiction in the name of helping him or her. One mother who bought her daughter's drugs so that she would not risk her life by going to dangerous places. In the name of "helping" her daughter, she was keeping her daughter sick. These family members claimed that love was the reason they did the silly, stupid things they did, helping the addict continue in his or her downward spiral. It was quite a metaphor for life.

There is no healing in sin. If people are going to get better, they have to face their sins, repent and allow Jesus Christ rebuild their lives from the inside out. Those who think they are being compassionate to divorcees by ignoring biblical standards are actually aiding and abetting the destruction of their lives. True healing comes when we face sin and bring it to Christ. Compromising biblical standards may make people feel better about themselves for a time, but it does not bring real and lasting healing. The compassionate view, while noble at heart, must be rejected because it does not bear eternal fruit.

The Redemptive View

In between the two points we have defined there are a host of views. This book will articulate a view called, the "Redemptive View." That word is rooted in the work of the Cross of Christ. It recognizes both the reality and effects of sin and the renewal and restoration of Christ. Jesus died to bring us new lives, to save us from the power of sin and to prepare us for an eternity in heaven, but also to transform our lives on a daily basis. Salvation is not only about the past and the future, but also about the present. The biblical teaching on divorce, remarriage and ministry reflects the overall themes of Christ's sacrifice, forgiveness, and redemption.

This view does not ignore the standards of the Scriptures. We must uphold the biblical ethic – one man, one woman, pure before marriage, faithful after marriage, "till death do us part." The Creator's intent was for monogamous and lifelong marriage and we must seek to honor that standard. On the other hand, even Jesus admitted that in this sinful world the ideal is not always real. Because of the sinful hardness of man's heart, God has made some exceptions to the rule of permanent marriage. Adultery. Abandonment. There are reasons why the faithful believer may choose to end a marriage in divorce. And where there is sin, God's grace abounds. We allow alcoholics to become pastors and church leaders, after God has rebuilt their lives. Many pulpits today are filled with people who engaged in premarital sex, but then experienced God's cleansing power. Every pastor, every deacon, every church elder is a sinner who has been forgiven, renewed, and had his character reconstructed by God. Our attitudes toward divorce should reflect that same redemptive work of Christ. The redemptive view of divorce seeks to combine a high view of marriage as lifelong and the reality of life in a broken world.

Leadership in the church is a matter of character and integrity. Those who lead the church must have spiritual integrity in their walk with Christ and must have demonstrated character to the church and community in their public walk. We are all sinners, though that sin takes different forms. God is working to conform us to the image of Christ. Those who lead the church are those who have advanced in that process of Christlikeness to the point that they can lead others in the process.

What matters is not what I did or who I was 20 years ago, but what I am today through the work of Christ. Maybe 20 years ago I was a drug dealer or a bank robber, or immoral. But today I am walking with Christ and people have grown to trust what God in doing in me. Leadership is not about what I was in my sin, but what I am in Christ.

Divorce should be treated no differently than any of these other sins. If I am in the middle of a divorce, I am not ready to be a leader in the church even if I am the "innocent party" in the dissolution. If I was divorced 25 years ago, remarried and in the intervening years have repented, had my life and character rebuilt by the power of God, and have demonstrated to the church the transforming work of Christ, ought I be treated as eternally defective? Should what happened 25 years ago eliminate me from service today? Are we not denying the redemptive and transformational power of Jesus Christ when we say that the sin of divorce is a permanent black mark? The denial may be unintentional, but it is nonetheless real.

Of course, arguments do not win the day; exegesis does. If the biblical evidence supports the prohibitionist view, then my view ought to be rejected. If "husband of one wife" really does mean "never divorced" then my view is wrong. But those decisions ought to be based on the accurate exposition of Scripture, not what we have always believed.

Toward a Biblical View

If we desire to develop a view of divorce, remarriage and ministry that is based on the biblical evidence, then there are some simple commitments that each of us must make. There are certain attitudes and priorities that tend to lead to biblical answers and others that do not. I believe that those who hold to the other views will agree on these points, even if they end up with different conclusions than I do.

To find the biblical position on divorce and remarriage issues, we must:

1. Observe the Scriptures with an open mind.

Have you ever seen the YouTube video where you are asked to count the number of times a ball is passed between the people who are on screen? I watched it and carefully counted the number of passes (as I recall, it was 14). At the end, the narrator asked if you had seen the man in the gorilla suit walk through the picture. I had not! The video was replayed and there it was, a man in a gorilla suit walking through the picture as clear as day. But I was so focused on counting passes that I did not see it.

It is easy to do that in the study of the Bible, especially if you have grown up in a church with strong traditional values. You hear something over and over again and you begin to assume that it is exactly what is taught in Scripture. Then, one day, you suddenly realize that your preconceived notions may not be what is revealed in God's Word. We can read things in that the Bible does not actually say and ignore teachings that are clear as crystal. We get so wrapped up in our preconceived ideas that we don't see the gorilla of truth walking through the text!

So, as we come to the study of God's Word, it is important that we lay down our preconceptions and traditional interpretations to ask ourselves what the Bible actually says. Dr. Howard Hendricks taught a seminary class called "Bible Study Methods" that changed my life. He pointed out that the key to Bible study was observation – taking the time to look and see what the Bible actually said before we try to interpret and apply it. That is key here. We must observe the full range of the Bible's teachings on divorce if we are accurately interpret them.

2. Look at all the scriptural evidence.

It is not enough to find one verse or two that seem to support your view and stick your finger in your ears, refusing to listen to what any other verses say. That is how so many theological and biblical arguments are conducted. Each side grabs a few verses that seem to support their position and ignore or discount those texts that seem to support the other side.

If the Bible is the Word of God as we believe it is, then there ought to be a consistency of the revelation concerning divorce and remarriage. For a view to be biblical, it must be in line with all the biblical evidence, not just a few verses. The teachings of the Old Testament will provide the foundation, which will be built upon by the words of Jesus himself, and be brought to completion by the teachings of the Epistles – a progressive revelation of the full will of God. Our doctrine must be built on a systematic and consistent exposition of all the biblical evidence

3. Ask the right questions.

As we examine the Bible's teachings on marriage and divorce, we will be focusing on and asking three primary questions. First, is divorce ever permissible for an obedient believer? Or, to put it another way, is divorce always sin? Are there situations in which a divorce can occur without sin? Second, is a divorced person ever allowed to remarry after a divorce? Is remarriage always adultery? Finally, are divorced people disqualified from leadership positions in the church, such as pastor, elder or deacon?

Methodology of This Study

This study will begin with an examination of the key passages in the Old Testament that discuss divorce. Next we will examine the teachings of Jesus, based on the Old Testament law, about marriage and divorce. Then we will turn our attention to Paul's teachings on the topic, primarily focusing on 1 Corinthians 7, the most extensive teaching on the subject in Scripture. After each of these segments (Old Testament, words of Christ, and Paul's teachings) there will be a summary statement and a general summary at the end. Finally, we will examine specifically the question of the fitness of the divorced for ministry positions in the church.

In this study, the primary contrast will be between the redemptive view and the prohibitionist view that is so common in the church. The compassionate view may be mentioned from time to time but will not be a main focus. Those who adopt that view tend to focus mostly on the hurts and healing of people, not on Scripture exegesis. Our debate will be centered on whether the Scriptures support the redemptive or prohibitionist views.

A Mnemonic Metaphor

We will begin this study by working through the scripture passages that deal with the topic of divorce and remarriage, developing a coherent biblical theology on the topic. Then, we will turn our attention to leadership issues, and whether divorced men are disqualified from leadership positions in the church.

We will use a metaphor to help remember the basics of the biblical teaching on divorce, remarriage, and ministry, an ancient building. Those buildings were begun with a cornerstone, then a foundation on which to build the structure. Then the building itself was constructed and finally the finishing touches were added to the structure. Cornerstone. Foundation. Structure. Finishing Touches. That's the basic outline of God's revelation on this topic.

The cornerstone of God's word on this topic is Genesis 2:24, which establishes marriage as a lifelong covenant between one man and one woman. The foundation is laid in Deuteronomy 24:1-4 where Moses, based on what Jesus called "the hardness of man's heart." Divorce needs a ground, based in the sinfulness of human beings. This is undefined in Deuteronomy, but the concept is introduced, laying the foundation for the New Testament teachings. Jesus erects the structure of the teaching in Matthew 19:3-12, along with his teachings in Matthew 5, and in Mark 10:1-12 and Luke 10:18. Paul then put the finishing touches on the construction project in 1 Corinthians 7, the most complete teaching in God's word on the topic of divorce and remarriage.

Once that building is fully constructed and we have a fully orbed understanding of God's revelation on divorce and remarriage, we will then apply those principles to the issues of 1 Timothy 3 and Titus 1, defining what it means to be "the husband of one wife."

Now, let us open our Bibles and begin to see what it says about divorce, remarriage, and ministry.

Cornerstone and Foundation: The Old Testament Evidence

Setting the Cornerstone and Laying the Foundation for the Biblical Teaching of Divorce, Remarriage, and Ministry.

That is why a man leaves his father and mother and is united to his wife, and they become one flesh. Genesis 2:24

Chapter 2: Old Testament Evidence

Here in Iowa, when we build a building, we dig deep footings to get below the permafrost, then we pour a foundation on which to set the structure. In ancient days, the practice was often to set a large cornerstone, then foundation stones were set that rested on the cornerstone. The cornerstone and the foundation stones provided the firm footing for a strong building. This is the picture used when Jesus is described as the Cornerstone. In our study, we will look to the Old Testament for both the cornerstone principles and the foundational truth that provides a firm footing for New Testament's full revelation about divorce, remarriage, and ministry.

The Law of God given to the Hebrews was radical in its treatment of women. Women did not generally have a place of prominence in Ancient Near Eastern society. They were essentially glorified slaves, property bought from the father, and replaced at the whim of the husband. Divorce was easily available to men at their whim and pleasure. A well-known Jewish tradition permitted a man to divorce his wife for burning his food. The woman had no right to divorce, any more than a slave could sell his master. Men were free to use or abuse their wives as they desired. God's Law gave protection to women and limited a man's right to treat his wife capriciously or with cruelty.

Biblical teachings on marriage and divorce must be seen against that background.

One note on methodology is needed. We are going to look at the Old Testament evidence on divorce, but not in chronological or biblical order. We are looking at them in an order that seems logical to the author in laying down the fundamental Old Testament teachings on divorce.

God's Original Intent

A Blessed Partnership – Genesis 2:24

That is why a man leaves his father and mother and is united to his wife, and they become one flesh. Genesis 2:24

In Genesis 2:24, we see the original revelation of God's intent for marriage. Humanity has strayed far from this intent, into immorality, into perversion, into corruptions of God's plan, but it remains God's perfect design. A man was to separate from his parents to partner with his wife and become one with each other. In God's paradise, marriage would have been a satisfying and pleasurable partnership and divorce would have been unthinkable.

Unfortunately, sin entered God's world and messed up God's perfect plan. The world became corrupt with sin. There is no record of the first divorce, but it is clear that divorce is a result of the fall of man into sin. Sin cursed the physical world with all sorts of disasters; it cursed men with fruitless toil, women with pain in labor; it cursed the spirit of man with death; and it cursed marriage with incompatibility, competition, strife and eventually divorce.

While neither of these points is germane to this discussion, two things are evident from this passage. First, polygamy was not part of

God's created order. A man was to leave home and marry "his wife." One. While in the fallen world it became a reality and it seems that God tolerated it among his people in the Old Testament era, it was never his desire and by the time of the New Testament it was clear that monogamous marriage was God's plan. Second, a man was to leave his parents and unite with his wife. Man and wife. Homosexuality was also not part of God's created order. The church ought to minister graciously to those who struggle with homosexuality, with compassion and kindness, but we can never approve of that which the Scripture does not. No matter how you slice the biblical evidence, you cannot make it support same-sex marriage.

The key teaching here is that marriage was meant to be a blessed partnership, not open warfare. God meant for a man and woman to become one – united in body, in soul and in spirit. A man was to leave his family and join to his wife and they would form something new. Marriage has strayed so far from the biblical ideal of one flesh, of a blessed partnership, that people instinctively seek to avoid it, as if it robs them of joy and of the vitality of life. God's intent in creation is still the biblical ideal, the plan of God – two individuals uniting to become one and being mutually blessed by that union.

Hear this as a word of hope from God. This book will deal with something brutal, the severing of one person (the two become one) into two. God did not intend people once united in marriage to be torn apart and it cannot be done without violence to the soul and spirit. It will be depressing to talk about divorce and it is gut-wrenching to deal with a family in the middle of the "one becoming two." Hear this, though, God's ideal stands and the power of God is still real. There is always hope. God is on the side of lifelong, blessed, contented, fulfilling marriage. If two people will give themselves to God and to each other, God becomes their ally in making the marriage work. God has healed marriages that were on the precipice of divorce and brought them back to joy and to hope. God does that. His arm is not short and his plan is not obsolete. There is nothing easy about marriage, done God's way, in this modern world where everything about biblical marriage has been rejected and written off as outdated and archaic. But we are not alone in the world. We have the power of Almighty God at work in us to sustain us and help us.

No marriage in this fallen world will be perfect, but God is at work to rebuild what sin has broken. Marriage is still God's will and He blesses those who seek Him in it. What we see most clearly in Genesis 2 is God's intent – that a man and a woman will join together in marriage, spend their life together, bound by both commitment and joy, serving him as one. This was his intent at the beginning, it is God's intent today and it will be until the end of time.

What does that mean about divorce? Divorce was never the intent of God for a marriage. Divorce is a fruit of the sin our ancestors brought into this world when they nibbled that fateful fruit. God's original intent is that a marriage last a lifetime and be blessed and that he is at work in those who seek him to enable that to take place. Divorce is not part of God's original plan and is only part of this world because of the sin we brought into this world.

Principle 1: God's original plan was and is lifelong marriage.

God's Attitude toward Divorce

If divorce was not part of God's creation, does that mean that it is always sin? What is God's attitude toward divorce? Many would seek to begin and end the discussion in Malachi 2:16 which, in the King James Version, records God saying, "I hate divorce." Nothing could be clearer, could it? If God hates divorce, it is a sin, a wicked thing.

There would seem to be little need to enquire further if God has spoken so clearly.

Unfortunately, I would argue that the clarity there is based on a mistake by the translators of the King James Version of the Bible and that the biblical evidence is much more nuanced than a simple declaration against divorce. Certainly, divorce is always a sign of failure. Two people who are walking in obedience to Christ do not get divorced. If a divorce takes place, someone has sinned, sinned deeply, and the plan of God has been disrupted. But that does not mean that every single person who is involved in a divorce is committing sin. Nor does it mean that there is no circumstance under which a person may seek a divorce. The sum total of scripture must be balanced here to discern the full and nuanced view of divorce and remarriage that is revealed there.

Since I asserted that the translation of the King James in Malachi 2 was not accurate, perhaps we should begin there as we seek to formulate a biblical view of divorce. We have established that it was not part of God's original plan and that it came in after the fall. But what is God's view of divorce now in this fallen world?

God Hates Divorce? – Malachi 2:10-16

"For the Lord, the God of Israel, saith that He hateth putting away; for one covereth violence with his garment," saith the Lord of hosts. "Therefore take heed to your spirit, that ye deal not treacherously." Malachi 2:16 KJV

"If he hates and divorces his wife," says the LORD *God of Israel, "he covers his garment with injustice," says the* LORD *of Armies. Therefore, watch yourselves carefully, and do not act treacherously. Malachi 2:16 CSB*

This verse has been used frequently as an absolute statement of God's opinion of divorce – that it is always a sin. "God hates divorce."

If a clear denunciation of divorce comes from the mouth of God, the debate ends. One major commentator says that this passage is the foundation for a biblical view of divorce, because God states unequivocally, "I hate divorce." And he does. When there is a divorce, it is clear evidence that someone has violated his revealed will and it is a tearing apart of two people that God has made one. Divorce brings brokenness and pain. All of this grieves the heart of God. He hates sin and all its effects. But is this passage saying what so many have said it is saying and is it accurate to extrapolate from this passage a general and universal prohibition of divorce?

It is not.

First, we must understand the context of this passage; no verse of Scripture is properly understood outside of its context. This passage is not talking about divorce as a theory but is addressing a specific and particularly heinous form of divorce. Men were leaving their Israelite wives and marrying Canaanite women, women who would lead them into idolatry. It was the pattern Israel had followed in the period of the Judges and Kings, the pattern that had brought Israel to destruction and to the Babylonian exile, and God did not want that to happen again. The sin here was not just divorce, but the breaking of the covenant with God and the embracing of idolatry. These Israelite were flirting again with the idolatry that had led previously to Israel's destruction. This was the sin that the prophet confronted.

It is hermeneutically suspect to make a verse this specific the formative verse for all the Bible's teaching on divorce. Frankly, the only real reason to do that is the fact that it fits people's views and says what they want it to say (in the KJV). If I want to advance a prohibitionist view of divorce, I might be tempted to elevate the importance of this verse beyond what it deserves. But even if "I hate divorce" were an accurate translation and interpretation of the verse (I will argue it is not) the fact that the context of the verse is so specific makes using this verse as the foundation for the Bibles entire teaching on the topic a questionable choice.

The King James translation which has God saying "I hate putting away (divorce)" is not an accurate translation of this verse. That is not what the Hebrew says and newer translations have almost uniformly given better renderings of the verse. The quote, "I hate Divorce" is a bad translation of what the original Hebrew said. Newer translations have given better renderings of the verse. It is a complicated construction, not easy to translate, but there are a few things we can deduce.

Let us begin with our conclusion, then seek to prove it. A better translation of this passage would be, *"For he who hates (his wife) to (the point that) he divorces (her), says the Lord, covers his garment with violence..."*

First, God is talking here, but the verb "hate" is a third person verb, "he hates." It seems clear that God is not the subject of verb, or he would say, "I hate." It is not God who is hating divorce, but a man who hates his wife to the point that he divorces her. After the opening conjunction, the verse has three verbs in a row. "For he hates to divorce, says the Lord." The verbs "hate" and "divorce" mostly likely identify the man who is the subject of the main clause later in the verse, "covers his garment with violence." Divorce is not the object of the verb hate here, but a second verb. "He hates, he divorces." This verse is not expressing God's view of divorce but is identifying the sinner — the one who hates and divorces his wife and covers himself with sin.

The first verb, "hates" is a different verb than was used in Malachi 1:3 (Esau I hated). This verb is more visceral. It speaks to someone having an emotional disgust. In this context, it refers to a man who treats his wife as if she were refuse, throwing her away in divorce to marry a Canaanite woman. This man has made a marriage covenant but treats his wife like something of no consequence (hates her) and violently throws her away, covering himself with sin.

God is calling this sin. Does God hate this behavior? You betcha! Those who perpetrated this sin were being called to judgment. The verse does not, however, give a blanket prohibition of divorce as the KJV seems to imply and the sin at hand is specific and heinous. A man who treats his marriage vows as nothing, who treats his wife as garbage, tosses her aside and goes after another is guilty of sin. This was true in the Old Testament and the New Testament and today. The breaking of the Mosaic covenant was especially heinous, but the sinful act remains sinful today.

The point is that it is clearly not the authoritative, comprehensive, universal condemnation of divorce that some prohibitionists have made it. That is an exegetical failure and a hermeneutical stretch.

Some readers are bothered now by the "reinterpretation" of Malachi 2:16. I would only encourage the reader to "search the Scriptures" and check what I am saying. I believe the KJV translation was wrong and this is correct according to Hebrew grammar.

If that bothered you a little, the next section, an examination of Ezra 9-10, will perhaps blow your mind. It is also a specific situation and we will not make universal applications, but the principle drawn from this passage is key.

God Commands Divorce – Ezra 9-10

Let us therefore make a covenant before our God to send away all the foreign wives and their children, according to the counsel of my lord and of those who tremble at the command of our God. Let it be done according to the law. Ezra 10:3

The situation here is similar to the one in Malachi 2, in which Israelites have left their wives to marry foreign women. This was prohibited in the law because it always led to the Israelites also leaving behind fidelity to God. When they married Canaanite women they also worshiped the Canaanite gods. And, as in the Malachi passage, this infuriates the Jealous God of Israel who demands that we love him with all our heart and soul and strength. In Ezra 10:3, God gives a command to those Israelites who have married the Canaanite women. God commanded that the foreign women were to be sent away (divorced). I will not attempt to draw any universal or eternal principle from this, but this simple fact is unmistakable and undeniable.

God commanded divorce.

If these men were going to be right with God, they would have to divorce the foreign women they had married. Scramble those eggs any way you will, but that is how the omelet is served. God commanded the Hebrew men to divorce. Was this a unique situation? Of course. Just like Malachi 2:16 was a unique (and very similar) situation. But you cannot leave Ezra 10:3 and say that divorce is wrong 100% of the time. At least once in human history it was the will of God. In this instance, it was not a sin to get a divorce, it was a sin not to get a divorce. To remain married to the Canaanite woman was the sin.

For those who would advocate a prohibitionist position, this verse has to be troubling. If divorce is always a sin, was God commanding Israel to sin? At the risk of absurdity, why in Jeremiah 3 and Isaiah 50:1 does God describe himself as giving a divorce to Israel if divorce is always a sin? It seems we must at least conclude that while divorce is never God's plan, and would not take place if people walked in obedience, it is not universally sinful either.

The Point

An important point emerges which lays the groundwork for our larger point and becomes fundamental in our later arguments. We saw in Genesis 2:24 that marriage was meant to be a lifetime partnership that brought joy and fulfillment to both partners. In a perfect world divorce would not exist. A man would treasure his wife and a woman would love her husband. They would live together in joy as God intended, partnering in life until death parted them.

Our world is not that perfect world – sin has broken what God made. While God's power can still work in the redeemed to create healthy marriages, and even rescue marriages from the brink, sometimes the ideal is not possible. And in a broken world sometimes you have to make tough choices; sometimes you have to make the best of a bad situation. Jesus said that God made certain allowances about marriages because of the hardness of the human heart. In a sinful world, the ideal sometimes is not the real and we must make hard choices to do the best we can in the real world. The Israelite men had to choose to divorce Canaanite women, even though God was normally opposed to divorce. But in that situation, the threat of idolatry was worse that the horror of divorce and the pain of the broken families. Because of sin, because of previous bad choices, because of the brokenness of the world, they were left with tough choices in less-than-ideal situations.

Please hear what I am about to say. I am not saying that because the world is sinful we should make divorce the easy way out. NO! NO! NO! Please do not infer that I am saying that if you are in an unhappy marriage, if you don't think you can be happy with your current spouse, if you are struggling to make things work and you don't feel like it's worth it, maybe you should just chalk it up to life in an imperfect world, cut your losses, move on and hope your next marriage is better than this one. That is not what I am saying. Not at all.

Our God is powerful and strong and even in this sin-soaked world he can bring glory from the ashes. Never give up on the power of God! He is able to bring marriages back from the brink, to enable forgiveness and restoration and to renew love. But there are times in this broken world when the miracles don't come and tough choices have to be made. A woman in an abusive marriage, or whose children are being abused, must make some broken-world choices. The spouse of a serial-cheater has to make some broken-world choices. When he leaves and doesn't come back, she is confronted with broken-world choices she cannot avoid. When she is through and wants out, and he has tried everything he knows how to try and has cried his eyes out and prayed his heart out, all that remains are broken-world choices. It is wonderful when God fixes everything. He can and sometimes he does. When it doesn't happen, we are left to make choices like the Israelites had to make in Ezra 10, to do something ugly to avoid something uglier.

This is the groundwork for the biblical teachings on divorce. Jesus would build on the passage we will examine in Deuteronomy 24 and he allowed divorce based on adultery. Paul would later add an exception based on abandonment. These were both rooted in the hardness of the human heart. No marriage is beyond God's power to heal and restore, but if a man or woman refuses to repent and embraces infidelity, that marriage may be irretrievably broken. If that man or woman abandons the marriage, it is not possible for the abandoned spouse to continue the marriage alone. I'm skipping ahead here, but I want the reader to see why I think these passages are important. In this wicked world, the wonderful ideal of God designed in Eden sometimes becomes impossible. God ordered the men of Israel to do one unfortunate thing – to divorce their Canaanite families – to avoid returning to idolatry, something God saw as even worse. In the real world, sometimes terrible decisions, broken-world decisions, have to be made.

Principle 2: In a broken world, broken-world choices are sometimes necessary.

Chapter 3: The Foundation: Deuteronomy 24:1-4

If a man marries a woman, but she becomes displeasing to him because he finds something improper about her, he may write her a divorce certificate, hand it to her, and send her away from his house. 2 If after leaving his house she goes and becomes another man's wife, 3 and the second man hates her, writes her a divorce certificate, hands it to her, and sends her away from his house or if he dies, 4 the first husband who sent her away may not marry her again after she has been defiled, because that would be detestable to the Lord. You must not bring guilt on the land the Lord your God is giving you as an inheritance. Deuteronomy 24:1-4 HCSB

It was not a great thing to be a woman in Ancient Semitic cultures. Regarded as property, they were servile and granted few rights or privileges. The Old Testament Law can seem harsh and oppressive as regards women, but seen against the backdrop of the times, they become almost radical. In that era many of the teachings that seem harsh to us were liberating, granting social standing to women and offering protection that they did not otherwise have. Many laws that seem repressive to us were actually designed to prevent men from arbitrary or cruel treatment of women. This passage, Deuteronomy 24:1-4 is such a text.

The fact that these four verses are the most comprehensive instruction in the Old Testament on the topic of divorce demonstrates how little the law spoke to the issue. I is a significant passage, because the principles that Moses lays down are key to the biblical revelation. Genesis 2 is the cornerstone, revealing God's intent for marriage to be a lifelong and joyous partnership. Deuteronomy 24 is the foundation that lays the groundwork for Jesus' teaching on marriage, divorce and remarriage. Paul, primarily in 1 Corinthians 7, but also in other passages, provides the finish work.

This passage is not about divorce, but about remarriage – it prevents Israelite men from divorcing a woman and remarrying her repeatedly. Men in that time had nearly unfettered discretion to divorce and to remarry. Women had no such right. Divorce was simple – no long and drawn-out legal process or division of assets. A man simply renounced his wife publicly and she was sent packing. He could later remarry her again, even if she had been married to another and divorced. This game of musical wives could proceed at the whim of the men involved with little regard to the feelings or well-being of the women. Women existed, they thought, to serve and please men. Deuteronomy 24:1-4 expressed God's displeasure at such practices and established a law in Israel that a man could not remarry a woman he had divorced once she had remarried another man, even if she were widowed or divorced again. This passage protected women by making a man think twice. He could not willfully send a woman away, because if he did, he might not ever get her back. He should not simply act on his whims and risk making impetuous mistakes.

That is the main point, but there are several other truths we may derive from this passage that become key in later biblical teachings and form the foundation of Jesus' teachings on divorce. To mix a metaphor, these are the roots from which the New Testament teachings on divorce and remarriage grow. I would call the reader's attention to three in particular.

Grounds for Divorce

The radical part of Moses' teaching on divorce is the establishment of the need for some cause on which to base a divorce. A man ought to have some legitimate reason to seek a divorce, not just a whim or a moment of petulance. In the patriarchal cultures of that day, men generally did not need any grounds. If they were tired of a woman, if she no longer pleased him, she could be sent away. Here, Moses demanded a cause, a reason, what we call "grounds for divorce."

Moses established that a man should divorce a woman only if he found a serious flaw in her moral character, what he calls in verse 1 "something improper." Other translations refer to "something indecent." Since he had made a covenant with his wife and with God, he ought not break it without solid grounds.

What is the indecency that breaks the covenant of marriage? Defining that word is no easy task. The Hebrew word usually means "to expose the genitals" and is often translated "nakedness." In Genesis 9:22, Ham found his drunken father and "saw the nakedness of his father." There was shame attached to exposing the genitals. In Genesis 3:7, Adam and Eve realized their nakedness after they had sinned. Almost every other time the word appears in scriptures, it has this connotation – the shame that derives from exposing the genitals. There seem to be two connotations attached to the word – a sexual component and a sense of shame.

There are also times when the meaning of the word is metaphorical, and this may be one of them. It seems safe to assume that Moses is not saying that a man can only divorce his wife if she exposes herself in public. Though it would fit easily into Jesus' adultery exception in

Matthew if we defined this "indecency" as sexual immorality or adultery, this literal interpretation has one glaring shortcoming. There were already penalties in the law for adultery and they did not involve divorce. They were much harsher! The penalty for adultery was death, as was just established in Deuteronomy 22:20-22. Why would Moses define adultery as a capital offense in chapter 22, then here offer it as the grounds for divorce? Something other than sexual immorality must be in view. Some have argued that this indecency only pertains to the initiation of marriage and refers to the lack of evidence that a woman is a virgin. However, in context there seems to be more at stake here than simply a maiden's failure to prove her virginity on her wedding night. The rabbinical schools of Hillel and Shammai argued over the meaning of this passage. The Shammai School took a more narrow view and the Hillel school a broad view. Those in the Hillel school maintained that a man could divorce his wife for any reason, even something as simple as burning his food. The meaning of this term was argued by them and by commentators on the Scriptures throughout the centuries.

After quite a bit of reading and study, I have come to a firm conclusion – I simply do not know what Moses meant by the term "something indecent." That may not be a satisfying answer, but to give anything more definitive would be to speak with more authority than is warranted by the evidence. Perhaps that is not such a bad thing. If we could define a specific character quality or activity as the subject of Moses' admonition, that would become our focus. But since we cannot, our attention can remain on the larger principle. Moses required a significant grounds for divorce, something that evidenced moral poverty and brought shame. A man couldn't divorce his wife because she packed on a few pounds or because he met someone new. He had to find a moral flaw to justify the divorce. We may never know what Moses meant, but we know that it did remove from the Israelite men the carte blanche to divorce their wives on a whim.

We can rely on the fact that in the New Testament both Jesus and Paul spell out the grounds for divorce more clearly, once the death penalty for adultery was no longer a reality as Israel's theocracy no longer existed. While we may have to leave some level of doubt about the meaning of the grounds for divorce in Deuteronomy, we are not forced to do so in the New Testament revelation. The Old Testament is unclear but the full revelation of Scripture leaves us without doubt as to what constitutes grounds for divorce.

Principle 3: Moses required moral grounds for divorce beyond a man's whims.

Process of Divorce

There is a second inference to be drawn from this passage, one perhaps with less import than the first. Moses established a formal process by which a man should divorce his wife. He could not simply send her away at whim, but had to give her a formalized certificate of divorce, a document that legally established her freedom from the marriage. This process is simple compared to the complexity of divorce today, but it was a formal process nonetheless. While this is not a huge issue, the content of that certificate of divorce is a significant factor.

Principle 4: Moses required a formal process of divorce.

Right to Remarry

One key question is whether those who divorce can remarry. In the biblical passages that deal with divorce, the right to remarry is assumed. This passage limits the freedom to remarry, but it is assumed that both the man and the woman will remarry after divorce. Jesus later puts more limits on remarriage, as will Paul. But as death ends a marriage, so does a biblically-justified divorce. When one divorces on biblical grounds, the divorcee is free to remarry.

The Mishnah is not scripture, but it gives us insight into the way the Hebrews practiced the teachings of this passage. The wording of this certificate that was used among the Hebrews is recorded there. "Let this be from me your writ of divorce and letter of dismissal and deed of liberation; that you may marry whatsoever man you will." A Hebrew man gave his wife this document freeing her from the bonds of marriage and giving her the freedom to marry "whatsoever man you will." This passage limits that right but assumes remarriage as the norm after a divorce. If remarriage were not the norm, why would the Law have to limit it in this way? There is a general assumption that the divorced will remarry.

A divorce which occurs according to biblical standards ends a marriage. Death is the only way God meant for a marriage to end, but in this sinful world, sometimes the hardened hearts of mankind lead to situations in which marriages do not last until death. When a marriage ends in divorce (assuming the New Testament conditions are met, since we live under those teachings), the marriage is over and the person who has been divorced is free to remarry. A biblically-sanctioned divorce is the severing of the marriage relationship and frees the person to remarry.

Principle 5: Remarriage is assumed after divorce, but is restricted.

Summary of Old Testament Teachings

The Old Testament teaching on our topic is brief, but it lays the foundation for the teachings of Jesus and Paul in the New Testament. The points made here in hints and foreshadows are expanded and expounded in the New Covenant teachings.

First, God's eternal ideal of marriage as a blessed lifelong partnership between a man and a woman.

Second, human sin can sometimes negate that ideal. In a world broken by sin, unfortunate choices must be made.

Third, in the Law, Moses established the need for legitimate grounds for divorce, limiting the rights of men to seek divorce arbitrarily or capriciously.

Fourth, Moses established a formal certificate of divorce.

Finally, remarriage is assumed as a product of divorce, unless that right is limited by God. Divorce did not free someone just to live single, but to seek another spouse.

These are the basic principles we can draw from the somewhat sketchy Old Testament evidence on divorce.

Building the Structure:
The Words of Jesus

Building the Structure of the Biblical Teaching on
Divorce, Remarriage and Ministry

But I say to you that everyone who divorces his wife, except on the ground of sexual immorality, makes her commit adultery, and whoever marries a divorced woman commits adultery."   Matthew 5:32

Chapter 4: The Words of Jesus

If anyone doubts that Jesus' teaching on divorce was shocking and new, look at the response of the men who listened to him give it. In Matthew 19:10, the disciples heard Jesus' teaching and responded that if that is right, "it is better not to marry." The idea of entering a marriage in which they did not have the right to send away the wife if she stopped pleasing him was inconceivable. They perceived wedding vows as responsive readings. The husband said "for better and the wife echoed, "for worse." If marriage did not serve a man's selfish needs why would he want to be in it at all?

Jesus' radical teachings on marriage and divorce were based on the passage we just studied, Deuteronomy 25:1-4. But Jesus built on that foundation in a way that shocked the "teachers of the law." He did not follow Shammai or Hillel but went a whole new direction that caused his hearers to be amazed and even to question the wisdom of marriage!

Deuteronomy 24 was a giant step forward from the culture in which the Hebrews lived, in that it put limits on a husband's right to divorce. He had to find a matter of some indecency. That standard was still nebulous enough that men were able to find a reason to get a divorce if they so desired. The husband had wide-ranging discretion and could give his wife a writ and send her away if she displeased him. Jesus moved the goalposts! He took divorce out of the whimsical subjective control of the man and established an objective standard. Christian men were only allowed to divorce a wife on the grounds of marital infidelity. Adultery broke the bonds of marriage and was the only exception Jesus allowed to his principle of lifelong union.

There are four passages in which Jesus refers to divorce, and all carry the same basic prohibition against divorce and remarriage. This is Jesus' first radical teaching, reestablishing God's original intent from Genesis 2:24 that marriage be a lifelong and blessed partnership between a man and a woman. There are some subtle differences in the four passages, so let us look at the biblical evidence.

Why the Differences?

Why does Matthew alone record the divorce exception, but Mark and Luke do not? In Matthew 5:31-32 (part of the Sermon on the Mount) Jesus lays down the standard that divorce is not permissible, except on the grounds of infidelity. Then, in Matthew 19:1-12 we see a lengthy exchange between Jesus and some Pharisees in which they discuss the Deuteronomy passage. Again, Jesus includes the adultery exception to the law of permanent marriage. Mark 10:1-12 is a separate account of what is clearly the same discussion. The two accounts are nearly identical, except that no divorce exception is mentioned. Luke 16:18 repeats the teaching of Mark 10:11-12 but does not include the context of the discussions, simply stating the teaching in a series of statements that confront the Pharisees. Only Matthew includes the adultery exception.

Many suggestions have been offered to solve this and we can easily dismiss some of them. If we accept the inspiration and inerrancy of

Scripture and honor its veracity and reliability, then we reject the notion that either Matthew or Mark and Luke simply got it wrong.

Others have attributed the adultery exception in Matthew to a textual error, suggesting that it was not part of the original text and was added later by a scribe to "clarify" the text. The problem is that the textual evidence is clear here. Matthew did include the exception in his original manuscript. The solution is not found in an appeal to textual variants. One could just as easily suggest that a textual error in Mark and Luke caused them to excise the exception.

The simplest explanation is probably the best one. Matthew and Mark both recorded accurately the teaching of Jesus, but neither was attempting to give a full transcript of the message. Read the Sermon on the Mount out loud. How long did that take? Do you imagine that Jesus' actual sermon was precisely that long, that what we have is an exact transcript of Jesus' message? Perhaps he spoke for hours. Different people could record different parts of the same speech, each accurately reporting what Jesus said, and yet not have exactly the same words.

Jesus gave the adultery exception in his teachings. Matthew recorded it. Mark did not. Mark was not trying to correct Matthew's teaching, nor was he denying that Jesus said it. Both texts are correct. Jesus said the words recorded in both. Matthew just records more of Jesus' said.

There words of Jesus in Matthew are the word of God and we must deal with them. The divorce exception cannot be denied by textual or other means. It must be dealt with exegetically, as part of the inspired, inerrant Word of God.

The Words of Jesus

In four passages, Jesus teaches about divorce. Our focus will be on the two passages in Matthew that deal with the divorce exception and we will only mention in passing the Mark and Luke passages, which are nearly identical to the Matthew passages, only deleting the exception.

Passage 1: Matthew 5:31-32

In Matthew 5, Jesus is explaining his role in fulfilling and surpassing the Old Testament Law. After establishing that principle he gives six examples of it. The Law prohibited murder, but Jesus raises that standard and includes the sin of anger in the heart. The Law restricted adultery, but Jesus sets a new standard, raising the bar to a standard none of us can keep. To even look on another with lust is to sin in the heart. He replaces the Lex Talionis (eye for an eye) with a new standard (turn the other cheek and go the second mile). He even would call on his disciples to love their enemies. Jesus took the Law and applied it to the heart. It was no longer about external behavior but about our minds, our souls, our inner beings. In that context, he tackles the Old Testament teaching, from Deuteronomy 24 and raises the bar on it as well.

> *"It was also said, 'Whoever divorces his wife, let him give her a certificate of divorce.' But I say to you that everyone who divorces his wife, except on the ground of sexual immorality, makes her commit adultery, and whoever marries a divorced woman commits adultery." Matthew 5:31-32*

He is calling his disciples to a higher life, a higher commitment to marriage than they have imagined. It is odd that today we look at this passage and focus on the exception – as if this passage somehow weakens the permanency of marriage by offering an exception in the case of adultery. Jesus was raising the bar on lifelong marriage in a way that freaked his disciples out! We will see in Matthew 19 how stunning people found this teaching. A follower of Jesus didn't just end a marriage with a certificate and send his wife away. Unless she broke the bonds of marriage through adultery, he was to remain committed to her, a "one-woman man" all the days of his life. Christian marriage is truly a unique and divinely inspired proposition.

Passage 2: Matthew 19:3-12

This passage deserves a closer look. The corresponding passage in Mark 10:1-12 is nearly identical, only eliminating the divorce exception. The teachings are identical. Luke gives the same teachings without the background details and also omits the divorce exception. We will focus our attention on the Matthew passage.

Jesus had left Galilee and gone down to the region of Judea, across the Jordan River. Large crowds followed him and he healed many. The Pharisees, always looking to undermine Jesus or trap him in some misspoken word, posed a question to him. "Is it lawful to divorce one's wife for any reason?" They were not asking if there was any reason at all for a divorce, but if a man had the right to divorce his wife for any reason he wished. They were, essentially, asking him to side with the Shammai or Hillel school. Jesus responded much like the angel did when Joshua asked him whose side he was on. The angel said, "I'm not on either side, I'm in charge." Jesus refused to side with either group, but established a new teaching that would render the discussion pointless. Rather than argue over what "some indecency" means in Deuteronomy 24, he established a new and clear standard.

Some Pharisees approached him to test him. They asked, "Is it lawful for a man to divorce his wife on any grounds?" *4 "Haven't you read,"* he replied, *"that he who created them in the beginning* **made them male and female,** *5 and he also said,* **'For this reason a man will leave his**

father and mother and be joined to his wife, and the two will ***become one flesh'?*** *⁶ So they are no longer two, but one flesh. Therefore, what God has joined together, let no one separate."⁷ "Why then," they asked him, "did Moses command us to give divorce papers and to send her away?" ⁸ He told them, "Moses permitted you to divorce your wives because of the hardness of your hearts, but it was not like that from the beginning. ⁹ I tell you, whoever divorces his wife, except for sexual immorality, and marries another commits adultery." ¹⁰ His disciples said to him, "If the relationship of a man with his wife is like this, it's better not to marry."*

¹¹ He responded, "Not everyone can accept this saying, but only those to whom it has been given. ¹² For there are eunuchs who were born that way from their mother's womb, there are eunuchs who were made by men, and there are eunuchs who have made themselves that way because of the kingdom of heaven. The one who is able to accept it should accept it." Matthew 19:3-12

Jesus responded to the Pharisees' question by taking them back to Genesis 2:24 to reestablish the divine intent of marriage. Divorce was not part of God's plan. He intended a man and woman to join together and stay married as long as they both lived. God takes this man and woman and joins them together as one. They are not two separate people anymore but one. This is a revolutionary, shocking teaching of Jesus in this passage. *"Do not divide what God has joined together."* God joins two people in marriage. Men do not get to divide into two what God has made one at their own whims. Sorry husband! When you marry, you are no longer in charge. Those men liked the idea that marrying and divorcing was completely at their discretion. They ruled their homes! But Jesus was teaching a different standard here. God ruled the home, not the man. Yes, a man is given leadership in his home, but only as one under greater authority. Biblical authority is always wielded under the greater authority of God! This was quite a blow to these men (as their reactions indicated). As a Christian man (women, too!), I walk under the authority of God! He joined us together and only he can separate us, when he calls one or the other of us to our eternal home. Marriage was designed by God to be permanent.

The Pharisees responded by appealing to Deuteronomy 24. They recognized that Jesus was superseding what Moses had taught. Look carefully at the wording of their question. *"Why then did Moses command one to give a certificate of divorce and to send her away?"* To them, this was a command of God, an expression of the way that things should be. A man should have an unfettered right to throw out a woman like she would an old piece of furniture. Jesus corrected that very quickly and made it clear that this teaching was not based on God's design but *"because of the hardness of your hearts."* Moses did not "command" divorce, but "permitted" it in special circumstances because of the effect of sin on human life. He then drives that point home. *"From the beginning it was not so."* Moses and the law may have permitted a man some freedom in seeking a divorce, but that was not the original intent of God when He created us male and female and ordained marriage on this earth. Divorce is always a deviation from God's original design, permitted only when sin has destroyed a marriage covenant. Sin causes divorce.

Then, Jesus laid out his radical new teaching. If you divorce and remarry except on the grounds of adultery, you become an adulterer yourself. Mark added that if your wife remarries, she will become an adulterer as well. It should be noted here that since Israel was no longer a sovereign nation, the Old Testament requirement of execution for adultery was no longer widely in place. The Jews could not execute without the permission of the Romans. Though the story of Jesus and the woman caught in adultery in John 8 indicates that they still considered stoning a possible punishment, it does not seem that it was widely practiced. The notoriously immoral Romans were not likely to sanction capital punishment for adultery. Jesus' point was clear – a new marriage is adulterous if the divorce was based on discretion not on adultery itself.

The disciples understood what Jesus was saying, but they did not like it. Jesus was taking marriage out of their hands, out of male discretion. Women were not under their thumb! Men and women were joined together under the hand of God and only he could sanction the dividing of what he had joined. God could break a marriage by taking one of the partners in death. And Jesus recognized that in a world broken by sin, adultery could break a marriage as well, and he authorized divorce (and remarriage) in that case. No matter how annoying, undesirable, nagging, unattractive, or bossy a wife became, a marriage was no longer under a man's discretion. It was under God's. It was a permanent decision, a lifelong covenant.

Even Jesus' disciples did not much like this teaching. You can imagine how the hostile Pharisees responded. Jesus went on to a rather strange discussion of being a eunuch, probably referring here symbolically to those who choose not to marry. He lays the groundwork for some of what Paul will later teach in 1 Corinthians 7. Marriage is a blessing from God and is sanctified by him, but singleness is also a blessed state for those who choose it.

Jesus concluded with an admission that we would do well to remember. This teaching will only be understood and applied by those "for whom it is intended." The people of God – the redeemed, Spirit-indwelled, Body of Christ – are the only people are who going to be able to fully accept and apply what Christ is teaching. As the world grows more sinful, we will see the teachings of the word less respected, more rejected. But we cannot reject what God teaches.

I performed a wedding in the summer of 2015 for a young couple who were vibrant Christians. As I prepared to address them, I had a realization. They were the future of the church! Young people who reject the sinful ways of the world and follow Christ with joy and fidelity. They will serve him, walk in his ways, raise a family to love him. They are the future!

What Constitutes "Adultery"?

A key question remains in this discussion. If Jesus permitted divorce only on the grounds of adultery, what constitutes adultery? Once, that question may have seemed straightforward, but in a nation that spent a year debating what the meaning of "is" is, we understand how difficult it can be. Is an "emotional affair" adultery? What about some of the practices that are so common today but do not involve sexual intercourse? What about a simple make-out session with someone you aren't married to? And cyber-sex – is that adultery? In this weird, perverted world, we have to ask and answer questions that previous generations did not even know existed.

The word in Matthew 19:9 is "porneia" and is a general and broad word used to describe all illicit sexual activity. Various attempts have been made to give this word a more specific meaning. Some say it only refers to immorality during the formal betrothal period, or the discovery that the wife was too close a relative to continue the marriage. The fact is that porneia is used in both those ways, but we cannot limit the meaning to a particular branch of illicit sex. Porneia included premarital sex, extramarital sex, homosexuality, bestiality, incest; any sexual act beyond the boundaries of marriage, the divinely ordained environment. Porneia is used to describe a life of wanton immorality, prostitution and general moral impurity.

There seems to be an implication, both in the word and in the Greek construction of this passage, that this porneia implies a continual lifestyle of infidelity which breaks the marriage bond and covenant. A single act of adultery is wicked, a breach of trust and a significant issue in the marriage, but Christians are called to forgive and seek restoration. The concept Jesus was teaching seems to be a willful, ongoing lifestyle of adultery that shatters the marriage bond beyond repair – a lifestyle of immorality that demonstrates that the marriage covenant has been irretrievably broken. A Christian is not looking for an excuse to get out of the marriage and relies on the power of God to rebuild and restore what sin breaks. He or she only invokes this exception as a last resort, when there is no hope, no other way. Jesus may have permitted divorce, but the Christian realizes that the glory of God is to work miracles of redemption and forgiveness, and goes down fighting for the sanctity and permanence of marriage. We must always remember the power of God!

What is the adultery that breaks a marriage? We must remember what marriage requires. As a husband, more is demanded of me than simply not having sexual intercourse with anyone other than my wife. Lust in my mind or heart is sinful as well. Fidelity encompasses more than simply avoiding intercourse with another woman. We must define what actions justify the divorce exception, what specific sins qualify as adultery. If my wife caught me looking at a scantily clad woman at the beach, she might be upset and I would have committed sin according to Jesus' words in Matthew 5, but no one would argue that justifies the adultery exception. If I was addicted to pornography, some say that qualifies, others do not. An emotional affair that does not become physical would be considered a violation by my wife, but would it justify her leaving me on the basis of the adultery exception? Cybersex in its various forms is clearly adulterous and evil, but whether it invokes the adultery exception is a point of debate. Any form of physical contact between a man and a woman (or, in this world, it must be said, a same-sex partner) of a sexual nature, seems to be a violation of that covenant, even if it falls short of intercourse. I have a wife. I am permitted to hold and kiss and touch her and only her – till death do us part. All other forms of romantic expression are forbidden, but at what point does that contact cross the line and become "porneia" that authorizes the adultery exception.

As a youth pastor, I would do lessons on the importance of sexual purity, and the first question would often be some variation on "Well, Dave, how far can we go?" I told them that when they were asking that question, they were headed in the wrong direction. The Bible is not about giving us strict rules to monitor our behavior but a holy walk with Jesus Christ. Our goal ought to be to please him and stay as far from sin as we can. The same concept is true as we approach defining porneia and the adultery exception. The Bible will not give us a clear rulebook that tells us precisely where the line is – stay on this side we are fine but put a toe across and the exception is activated. My desire as a husband should be to stay far from the adultery line.

I must never give my wife any reason to be insecure, jealous, or afraid. My commitment to being a one-woman man must be unshakable and obvious in all I do. I try to live that out every day not only by being technically faithful to her, but by avoiding intimacy of any kind with other women – physical, emotional, or spiritual. She must be the only woman I share my life with in any significant sense. A Christian husband does not see how close to the edge he can come, but stands strong in holiness and devotion.

A Christian husband or wife is not looking for an escape clause in his or her marriage. We are committed to lifelong marriage and so we are willing to forgive injuries, letting God bring healing and restoration to marriage, as hard as that is. Divorce is a last resort, when the other party has broken the marriage irretrievably and shows no willingness to repent and be restored. Drawing a clear line of adultery is not essential because we are not looking for an excuse to divorce, hoping for a spouse to put a toe over the line and invoke the clause. Only when a spouse rejects God's plan so totally that the covenant is irretrievably broken. Spirit-filled believers default to permanent marriage and only divorce when the other person makes it necessary.

Perspectives

1. Jesus left no doubt that the original intent of God was marriage that lasted a lifetime. One man, one woman; joined together by God for as long as life lasts. He established marriage as an institution ruled by God, and not by the whims of the husband.

2. Jesus established sexual immorality is the only grounds upon which divorce would be permitted, a lifestyle of unrepentant and willful adultery which breaks the marriage covenant irretrievably.

3. A divorce that is based on grounds other than adultery (specifically, the whims of a man) is sinful and any remarriage that follows from that is adulterous, since in God's eyes the first marriage is still in effect.

4. A Christian only seeks divorce as a last resort, not as a first option. The smallest act of infidelity breaks trust in a marriage, but we have the Spirit of God and through God's work in us, we can forgive and restore what sin has broken. One strike and you're out is not the way of those who have been redeemed by Jesus Christ.

5. Jesus told those who remarried after an unsanctioned divorce that they were living in adultery. The logical inference is that remarriage after a divorce that includes adultery is permitted and is not sinful. A

sanctioned divorce ends the marriage in God's eyes and that person is free to go on and marry another.

A note here related to gender is appropriate. In those days, only men were allowed to divorce, which is why the passage is written as it is. This should not be read as a teaching that only men have the right to divorce, but as a cultural accommodation. There is no reason why the principles taught by Jesus here should not apply equally to men and women in a culture in which both men and women are allowed to seek divorce. Paul later will expand on Jesus' teaching and grant rights to both men and women.

Jesus' teaching on divorce is shocking and revolutionary. He held up the original intent of marriage clearly and uncompromisingly. He also made a single exception to his rule of permanent marriage, adultery. In that case, divorce was permissible in God's eyes as a last resort.

Finishing Touches: Paul's Teachings

Putting the Finishing Touches on the Biblical Teachings
on Divorce, Remarriage, and Ministry

*For the unbelieving husband is made holy because of his wife, and the
unbelieving wife is made holy because of her husband...But if the unbelieving
partner separates, let it be so. In such cases the brother or sister is not enslaved.
God has called you to peace.*   *1 Corinthians 7:14-15*

Chapter 5: Paul's Teachings

Most of the Bibles I had growing up had the words of Jesus in red letters. It is a helpful study tool if you are looking to find something Jesus said in the gospels, but it can cause problems in Bible Study. Every word Jesus spoke was perfect, but the high view of inspiration that we hold extends that same perfection to the scriptures written by Paul, or Peter, or James, or John. The red words in John are no more inspired and no truer than the black words of Paul. The Jesus whose red words appear in the Gospels spoke through the other biblical authors as well. This becomes significant as we deal with the topic of divorce. Jesus spoke an authoritative and clear word on divorce, but it was not the final word. Paul expanded on Jesus' words in his writings, especially in 1 Corinthians 7. Those words are just as true and authoritative as the words spoken by the Savior himself.

The biblical revelation about divorce and remarriage is progressive. It began with Genesis 2:24, the cornerstone, which revealed God's eternal purpose in marriage – a lifelong and joyous partnership. Deuteronomy 24 laid the foundation, setting forth the principle that a man needed a legitimate reason to divorce his wife, "some indecency," and needed to follow the formal process God set out. Women were not just property to be treated on the basis of a husband's whims and desires but were to be respected and treated with dignity. Jesus took that teaching and built on it, transforming it radically in the process. He placed marriage in God's hand rather than simply in the husband's and restored the original intent of marriage – that it would be a lifelong partnership. Jesus did not allow a man to simply decide to leave his wife, but set an objective standard for divorce, adultery. A marriage could only be ended when adultery took place. Now, in Paul's teachings, the full revelation of God will be given, building on Jesus' words. Paul, in 1 Corinthians 7, will add one more exception to the adultery exception that Jesus gave, and deal with certain other scenarios that did not apply when Jesus was speaking. Paul did not change Jesus' words in any way, but simply built on them, expanded them, and finished them. There is no conflict between Paul's teaching and that of Jesus. They are in harmony.

Paul's words could not be any truer if they were written in red letters!

Paul's Viewpoint

It might surprise the American Christian to realize how little the New Testament says about marriage and family issues. Churches today give much greater time proportionally to preaching on the topic than the Scriptures did to revealing truth about them. I am observing a fact and drawing no specific inference from it. Fortunately, those teachings, though scant, are clear and consistent. Ephesians 5:22-33, Colossians 3:18-19, and 1 Peter 3:1-7 all instruct husbands and wives on their biblical roles. The husband is to love his wife as Christ loved the church and the wife is to submit to her husband in obedience to Christ. Men and women are equal before God – equally loved, equal in value, equal in Christ's kingdom, but we have differing roles in marriage.

Divorce is even less common a topic than marriage in the Epistles. In Romans 7:1-6, Paul uses divorce as an illustration of a believer's "divorce" from sin. In 1 Timothy 3 and Titus 1, leaders in the church are required to be "the husband of one wife." While the meaning of that phrase is in doubt, it is part of the discussion over divorce and remarriage. The most extensive teaching on divorce in the entire Bible is 1 Corinthians 7:10-24. Our study of Paul's teachings will focus on two areas. We will examine the 1 Corinthians 7 passage to see the full counsel of God on the topic of divorce and remarriage. Then we will turn to our original question, studying 1 Timothy 3 and Titus 1 to determine if men who have been divorced (or are married to women who are divorced) are disqualified from service as pastors, elders, or deacons in the church.

Is Paul's Teaching Scripture or Opinion?

First, though, we must address a question that has come up often in studies of 1 Corinthians 7. In verses 10-12, Paul makes comments that have led some to believe he is claiming that his teachings are either not inspired Scripture or have less authority than the words of Jesus in the Gospels. There was a new situation in Corinth – mixed marriages. Men and women were being saved and finding themselves married to unbelievers. Was that okay? Should a Christian share a bed with an idol worshiper? Perhaps God would be pleased if a Christian divorced such a spouse. What if the lost spouse was unwilling to live with the Christian? How should the Christian respond? In responding to these new situations, Paul gave this instruction.

To the married I give this command—not I, but the Lord—a wife is not to leave her husband. ¹¹ But if she does leave, she must remain unmarried or be reconciled to her husband—and a husband is not to divorce his wife. ¹² But I (not the Lord) say to the rest: If any brother has an unbelieving wife and she is willing to live with him, he must not divorce her.

What did Paul mean when he said, "I, not the Lord?" When he asserts that it is "Not I, but the Lord" speaking, there is little doubt what he is saying. He is referencing the Savior's words in the Gospels about the permanence of marriage as the authority for his own. Then he addresses "the rest" and admits that it is "I, not the Lord" who is giving this instruction. What is he saying? Is he, as some have claimed, admitting that this is his own opinion and should not be taken as having divine authority? Some prohibitionists take this view to explain Paul's teachings here which create new exceptions. "These were Paul's opinions but not divinely inspired." That view is convenient if what Paul teaches here does not fit your view of divorce and remarriage, but it carries a trainload of theological baggage. Chief among them is the idea that Paul would assert his own opinions that diverge from the authoritative teachings of Jesus Christ. "Here's what Jesus said, but here's my differing opinion." Paul would never do that. Such a view also conflicts with our cherished view that "all scripture is inspired and useful for teaching" (2 Timothy 3:16). Paul had too much respect for the inspired word than to insert his own opinions into such an instruction.

There is a much simpler solution here, one that does not slough off this text into the discard pile. Paul was making a distinction here, not between inspired instruction and his own opinions, but between the authoritative teachings of Jesus himself and the teachings that the Holy Spirit revealed directly to him. Jesus addressed marriage and made a single exception to the permanence of marriage teaching – adultery. Through Paul, God was now addressing a situation that was not extant when Jesus taught and was revealing a second exception to the law of permanence. As a marriage covenant could be broken by adultery, it could also be broken by abandonment. This teaching was not Paul's opinion, it was the revelation of God, carrying equal authority as the "red words" of Jesus, but it was given to Paul directly.

What God revealed to Paul was not in conflict with what Jesus had said. In essence, it was an expansion of the principle Jesus had taught. Jesus asserted that marriage was meant to be permanent – till death do us part. "What God has joined together…" Jesus recognized that, "because of the hardness of man's heart," there should be an exception made. The sin of adultery can break the marriage covenant. Through Paul, God simply applied that principle to another situation, a new situation the church faced as the gospel began to spread. Jesus had warned of the divisive effect of the gospel, even on families, and that was coming to pass. How should the church respond to this? Through Paul, the Spirit revealed precisely how such situations should be handled. It was an application of the same principles Jesus used to a new situation – under the inspiration of the same Spirit that filled and inspired Jesus.

In the Olivet Discourse in John 14-16, Jesus promised that the Spirit would come and reveal "all truth" to the church. Paul was the vehicle through whom the full truth of God's revelation on marriage, divorce, and remarriage was given and the prophecy of Jesus Christ in his final sermon before his crucifixion came to pass.

Paul's Teachings

Paul's teachings on divorce, remarriage, and ministry are not extensive. They are consistent with those made by Jesus in the Gospels but they expand on them. Paul affirmed the core teaching, that marriage is designed by God to be a lifetime partnership and that divorce should not be an easy way out, a first resort to solve unhappiness. His teachings are the culmination of biblical revelation on the topic. The cornerstone was laid in Genesis 2:24 and the foundation was poured in Deuteronomy 24. Jesus erected the framework in his teachings in the Gospels and now Paul does the finish work on the subject. We will examine three passages (four, actually, but the last two will be examined together). We will look briefly at the illustration Paul makes in Romans 7, then we will give a more in-depth examination to 1 Corinthians 7. Finally, we will study the teaching of 1 Timothy 3 and Titus 1 in which Paul says that elders and deacons must be the "husband of one wife" and seek to define that phrase.

Romans 7:1-6

Strangely, divorce and remarriage prohibitionists tend to discount the primary passages on the topic while elevating secondary passages to As noted previously, some have tried to assert that Malachi 2:16 is the foundational teaching in the entire Bible on the topic of divorce, when a proper interpretation of that passage renders that absurd. Others have tried to make this passage Paul's primary teaching on the topic of divorce, but that, too, is a hermeneutical error. This is not a passage about divorce, but is about sin and how our salvation frees us from sin and the law. People born in sin are bound to the law as a woman is bound to her husband. When her husband dies, she is free to remarry, but she is not free as long as he lives. In the same way, we are only freed from the law when Christ nullifies the penalty of sin and the power of death in us. This passage uses marriage as an illustration of freedom we have in Christ when we are "buried with Christ by baptism into death and raised to walk a new life in him."

An illustration is designed to make a point and it is a mistake to take that illustration and apply it beyond the point it is intended to make. The redemptive viewpoint I am arguing for in this book affirms that idea – a point that has been made repeatedly. Marriage was designed by God as a permanent covenant between a man and a woman. Humanity has found many ways to pervert and degrade God's idea through the years – homosexuality, polygamy, and of course, divorce. But God's intent did not change through all that time.

However, the fact that Paul made an illustration based on the divine intent of permanent marriage does not negate the rest of the scriptural teaching on the subject. His illustration here stands, but so does the fact that the hardness of the human heart has created a necessity for exceptions to be enacted. When one party to the marriage covenant irretrievably breaks that covenant by his or her sin, the other party is freed from the covenant the other has broken. It is bad hermeneutical practice to use an illustration such as Paul made in Romans 7 as a primary teaching. This is not about marriage and divorce. It is about the law, sin, salvation and the Christian life; marriage and divorce are only used for illustrative purposes.

Romans 7:1-6 adds little to the discussion of divorce and remarriage, other than to reaffirm the cornerstone principle of the biblical revelation – that God intended marriage to be a lifelong covenant.

I Corinthians 7:10-24

Robert K. Merton is credited with naming and popularizing the "law of unintended consequences." We act determined to accomplish certain purposes, but there are often other results that we did not anticipate that happen as well - unintended consequences. As the sovereign purposes of God are carried out in this sinful world, there are sometimes consequences that arise that must be dealt with, problems that, at least on a human level, could not be foreseen. As the gospel spread in the Roman world, lives were changed by the power of God, but there was some fallout as well, some issues that had to be addressed. These were not a surprise to God, of course. Jesus warned that he came to bring a sword and that he would divide families. That is exactly what was taking place in Corinth.

As the gospel spread, often only the husband or the wife would come to Christ. These were not nominal conversions, but people who gave themselves to Christ body, soul, and spirit. When one party in a marriage gave himself or herself fully to Christ, it had a marked impact on the marriage, causing real problems. Christians have a new purpose in life, a new outlook, new attitudes, new standards of behavior and new ways of relating to one another. Evidently, not all the lost spouses appreciated the changes Christ was making in their homes. An idol-worshiping husband might be offended when his wife identified his gods as false and wanted to destroy those idols to serve this Jesus. A wife, happy in her pagan ways, might not be thrilled to be the object of her husband's evangelistic efforts.

Some new Christian converts may have questioned whether it was right for them to share their lives and their bodies with someone who worshiped idols. If they were truly devoted to Christ, should they do as God commanded the Israelites in the Old Testament and separate completely from the "Canaanites" and their idolatry? Is it possible that stories such as those that we examined from Ezra where God commanded the Israelites to divorce their Canaanite wives were raising questions among these new converts to Christianity? In their passion to serve Christ, and perhaps the frustration in their unequally yoked marriages, questions were being raised, questions which Paul addressed here in 1 Corinthians 7.

Paul needed to address two questions. First, was it acceptable for Christian to remain in a marriage with a non-Christian, a pagan idol-worshipper? Second, what if the idol-worshiping non-Christian decided to leave? What responsibility did the Christian have then? A third question would follow. What if the non-believer did not leave, but created a hostile environment for the marriage? What should the

Christian do then? In this chapter, Paul would address all of these questions.

1 Corinthians 7 is the most lengthy and comprehensive teaching on the topic of divorce and remarriage in the entire Bible. It is the culmination of all that has gone on before (the Genesis 2:24 cornerstone, the Deuteronomy 24 foundation, the Gospel framework) and the only teaching that follows is Paul's instruction to the church about leadership, about elders and deacons being "the husband of one wife."

An Astounding Innovation

There is one huge innovation in this passage. Deuteronomy discusses a husband giving his wife a writ of divorce and the Gospel passages limit that, saying that a man can only divorce his wife on the grounds of adultery. In 1 Corinthians 7, for the very first time, the right to divorce is granted both to men and to women. There may be a cultural element at work here - pagan Greek culture was different than ancient Hebrew culture. It also represents the heart of God toward the fundamental equality of men and women. Contrary to how it is often portrayed, the essential equality of men and women is a bedrock principle of complementarian teaching. We believe that while God has given us different roles in certain institutions (in the church and at home), men and women are equally loved, equal bearers of the image of God, equal in the heart of God and of equal value to him. It is both a great blessing and instructive that in this ultimate lesson on marriage, divorce, and remarriage this equality is emphasized.

The Core Truth: Marriage is a Lifelong Covenant

Couples seldom sit in my office to be counseled for minor problems. By the time they come to me, the issues are severe and often my fleshly instinct is to think that it would just be easier to tell these two to cut their losses, go their separate ways, and try to start over and find happiness in new relationships. That advice is often given by those who do not hold fast to the teachings of the Scriptures. We cannot give in to this deceptive and easy road – fidelity to the Savior and his commands will not allow it. From the cornerstone in Genesis, to the foundation in Deuteronomy, through the structure built by Jesus Christ, and culminating in the full teaching here in 1 Corinthians 7, the principle of marriage as a lifelong covenant is the fundamental principle. Even when exceptions are given they do not negate the rule. God intends for ever marriage to last a lifetime and he empowers those who seek him to work through their problems and keep the fires burning "till death do us part." We cannot easily give up on marriages when the power of God is available to renew, restore and rebuild them. We must approach marriage from a supernatural perspective, as the work of God that they are.

On the Other Hand

The purpose of Paul's instruction in 1 Corinthians 7 is to address issues that had arisen as the gospel spread through the pagan world. Moses, Jesus reminded us, understood the hardness of the human heart and made allowance for it. Jesus did the same, providing an exception to the permanence of marriage if one party broke the covenant through adultery. Because of human sin, sometimes marriages fail and die. One person, even one walking by faith and obedience, expending himself or herself in fidelity to marriage, cannot stop a sinful spouse from breaking that marriage covenant and walking away. Moses knew that. Jesus knew it. And Paul devotes this chapter to dealing with circumstances in which one party's sin affects a marriage.

After beginning the chapter with a discussion of general principles of marriage, of the rights of husbands and wives over each other's bodies and the importance of meeting one another's sexual needs, he addresses the value of living single and establishes it as a viable and worthy option for those who are able to do it. Much could be written about these verses, but since this is a book focusing on divorce, remarriage, and ministry, we will begin our discussion in verse 10, where Paul turns his attention to marital problems and to divorce.

Establishing the Default (1 Corinthians 7:10-11)

In computer terminology, a "default" is a preselected option to which the computer automatically reverts unless it is instructed to do differently. It is the automatic option. For Christian marriage, we have a default option – permanent marriage. In verses 10 and 11, Paul establishes this general rule, which is little more than a restatement of the principles taught by Jesus, which he makes clear by giving credit to the Savior. Christians are not to initiate divorce or to make that our first option.

> *To the married I give this command—not I, but the Lord—a wife is not to leave her husband. ¹¹ But if she does leave, she must remain unmarried or be reconciled to her husband—and a husband is not to divorce his wife. ¹² But I (not the Lord) say to the rest: If any brother has an unbelieving wife and she is willing to live with him, he must not divorce her. 1 Corinthians 7:10-11*

This passage is meant to establish the basic principle that has been the core of every teaching on marriage since Genesis 2:24. For the moment we will ignore the parenthesis and simply examine the two declarations. A wife should not separate from her husband and the husband should not divorce his wife. God wants marriage to be permanent. If the reader wonders why I am repeating this message, it is not by accident. As we discuss exceptions to the permanence of marriage, as we talk about those times when God grants the right to seek a divorce, it can leave a wrong impression on some – that divorce is no big deal. Unhappy in your marriage? Walk away. Start over. God will forgive. He wants you happy after all. But nothing could be farther from the truth. Marriage is, always has been, and always will be a lifelong covenant intended by God to last till our final breath. If there are a few exceptions granted on the basis of the hardness of the human heart, that does not negate the rule. I repeat the principle often just so that principle is not forgotten in the discussion.

Paul tells wives that they should not separate from their husbands, and if they do separate, they should either remain single or seek reconciliation with their husbands. Men were given no leeway. They were not allowed to divorce their wives. This is not, as some have asserted, a command against all divorce, because Paul has referenced the Lord's teaching which allowed divorce on the basis of adultery and would go on in this passage to give another exception to the permanence of marriage. Paul's point here is more general. God intends for marriage to be permanent and a Christian husband or wife should not seek to end the marriage. It is simply not the act of a follower of Jesus Christ to seek an escape from our marriage vows. Our duty is to seek to heal and restore marriage, not end it. God graciously grants exceptions when the other party breaks the marriage covenant, but the Christian ought not be seeking a way out.

Paul's instructions here to men and women are slightly different. To men the command is absolute. A man must not divorce his wife, assuming that no exceptions exist. A similar teaching is given to the wife. She is not allowed to separate from her husband. The different terminology may recognize different legal realities in that world, in which only men had the privilege of seeking legal divorce. But she was not to walk away from her marriage.

This is where the first "exception" takes place in this passage. In our translation, the phrase is parenthetical. The wife is not to separate from her husband, but if she does separate from him, she must live as a single woman or seek reconciliation with her husband. Those are her only options. There are certain clear facts in this passage. A wife is given an option that is not given to the husband. The husband may never divorce his wife, but a wife, though told not to separate from her husband, is given the right to separate if she must. If she does separate under these circumstances, she is not free from her marriage vows and cannot remarry. She must either reconcile with her husband or she must live single.

This passage deals with the situations that are not addressed in the "exception" passages – either those addressed by Jesus or those addressed later in this passage by Paul. This is about what we would call incompatibility. A man cannot simply divorce his wife because she doesn't make him happy anymore, or because she has put on weight, or because she does not "do it for him" anymore. A woman cannot separate from her husband because he is not the Prince Charming she thought was waiting for her when she walked down the aisle. He is not as attentive, as kind and doting as she would like, perhaps, but that is not an excuse to walk away from the covenant she made before God.

However, the wife is given an exception here, an option to separate and live as a single woman. Why is a woman given that option when the man receives no such choice? It is because the Scriptures view the husband as the head of the home and grant him authority in that home. He has the power to set the tone and to try to make the changes necessary to build a happy and godly home. The wife, who is called to submit to her husband's authority, does not have that same ability to control the tone and temper of a home. If the husband creates an environment of hostility, hate, abuse, or even danger for the wife, she may decide that it is better to live as a single woman than to live under the authority of her husband. This is exception is given to the woman to protect her from a husband who abuses the authority that God has given him.

In a later chapter, we will explore in more detail the too-current issue of whether churches and pastors ought to counsel women who have been abused to stay with and submit to their abusive husbands.

It would be a mistake here, I believe, to use the prohibition on remarriage given to the wife in this specific situation as a general prohibition of remarriage in all divorces, as some have tried to do. The wife here is not divorcing her husband – in general, wives did not have that legal right. She is simply separating from her husband. She is still legally married to him, so of course she cannot seek another marriage. That would be adultery. A divorce ends a marriage but this is not a divorce, only a separation. As we established in previous studies, remarriage is the natural product of a biblically approved divorce.

The basic principle Paul taught was the same that has been taught throughout the Scriptures. Marriage is a lifelong covenant. Though he will now turn his attention to exceptions to that principle based on certain situations, the exceptions were not meant to nullify the principle. Marriage is a lifelong and committed covenant between a man and a woman.

Difficult Situations

Having reestablished the foundational truth of permanent marriage, Paul then deals with three situations which had arisen in Corinth and other areas where the gospel had advanced in the pagan world. Paul is breaking new ground, as he makes clear in verse 12, addressing topics which Jesus did not address. He deals with two situations that arise when one partner in a marriage is saved and the other is not, then he addresses how to deal with that which took place prior to salvation.

This would include both divorce and in some cultures in that world, polygamy.

If the Unbeliever Stays – 1 Corinthians 7:12-14

It is likely that confusion existed among new believers in places such as Corinth. Hearing the gospel, they gave themselves without reservation to Jesus Christ, renouncing all allegiance to the idols they had worshiped all their lives. They gathered with other believers to worship Jesus, to break bread and honor the Body broken and the Blood shed for their sins. Then, they came home to a spouse who still bowed down to idols and worshiped the false gods they had utterly rejected. Was this acceptable? Was it right to share a life and a bed with husband or wife whose heart did not share the most important passion of the new believer's life? And, perhaps, someone had pointed out the story we looked at in Ezra 9-10, in which God commanded the Hebrew men to divorce their pagan wives so as not to be led back into idolatry. It is easy to see how they could conclude that loyalty to Christ demanded that they leave their pagan spouses, especially considering that the Roman world did not have the same values regarding marriage that we are used to as Christians today – leaving a marriage did not have the same stigma that we might attach to it. So, that was the quandary the new believers of Corinth found themselves in, wondering if it was acceptable to stay in a marriage with a non-believer.

Paull addresses the situation in verses 12-14, turning the tables on the concept.

But I (not the Lord) say to the rest: If any brother has an unbelieving wife and she is willing to live with him, he must not divorce her. 13 Also, if any woman has an unbelieving husband and he is willing to live with her, she must not divorce her husband. 14 For the unbelieving husband is made holy by the wife, and the unbelieving wife is made holy by the husband. Otherwise your children would be unclean, but as it is they are holy. 1 Corinthians 7:12-14

No, Paul says, do not divorce your husband or wife if they are willing to stay, just because they do not share your faith. As a born-again, Spirit-indwelled, God-honoring presence in the home, you become an agent of God's work in that family, a tool for God to use in sanctification. My dad was saved out of a religious but largely unsaved family. Over the years, many others in his family came to Christ. He was the agent of God who "sanctified" his family.

The word "made holy" is means to set apart for God. One saved family member is the pathway through which God can work in other's lives. Believers should not divorce their unbelieving spouses to pursue spiritual purity but should seek to stay in those marriages as agents of God's grace. When one member of a family or one partner in a marriage is saved, it sets apart the whole family for the activity of God. Each of us must come to Christ on our own. No one inherits salvation and we cannot be saved by proxy, but the presence of one redeemed and Spirit-filled person in a family opens the door for God to work throughout the entire family.

If the unbeliever is willing to stay in the marriage, the believer should not end the marriage on the grounds of religious incompatibility but should stay and attempt to demonstrate the love and power of Christ to the rest of the family, to live the gospel and share it. Evangelism starts at home. Salvation does not vitiate the marriage vows but enabled the family to begin experiencing the grace of God. Christians, empowered by the indwelling presence of the Spirit, should be agents of reconciliation.

If the Unbeliever Leaves – 1 Corinthians 7:15-16

It boggles the minds of those of us who have been saved by God's grace through Jesus that everyone who hears the message does not respond, but many do not. In every church I have pastored, there have been redeemed wives with husbands who will not listen and (a few) redeemed husbands whose wives want nothing to do with the faith. A believer ought never initiate a divorce because a spouse is an unbeliever, but what happens when a person is saved, transformed, renewed, and the unsaved spouse hates what Jesus is doing? What happens when the unbeliever refuses to accept the new person Christ is creating and walks out the door? Jesus didn't address this in his earthly ministry – it would not have come up. But now, he addresses it by inspiring the Apostle Paul to address the subject. What happens when a Christian spouse is abandoned by the unsaved spouse? What should the redeemed do?

> But if the unbeliever leaves, let him leave. A brother or a sister is not bound in such cases. God has called you to live in peace. [16] Wife, for all you know, you might save your husband. Husband, for all you know, you might save your wife. 1 Corinthians 7:15-16

His instruction is clear. If a believer is abandoned by an unbelieving spouse, the believer is not "enslaved," not bound to the vow that he or she made and was willing to keep, but the other broke. God has granted to such a believer peace – the peace of freedom and release from the marriage, and the freedom to remarry. While a believer would be heartbroken in such a case, he or she should take comfort that there was no guarantee that they could have reached the other with the gospel. Rest in the peace of God, accept what you did not want.

This passage does not fit the prohibitionist's system easily and must therefore be made to say what it does not. Paul is calling the

Corinthians to live in peace and freedom. That does not mean that Christians can or should leave a marriage easily – we do not close the curtain and walk offstage when things get tough. In a fallen world, we recognize that there are situations over which we have no control. A believer who has been redeemed, who sought to glorify God but was rejected by his or her spouse need not spend the rest of his or her life in remorse and self-recrimination. A believer seeks to preserve the marriage and then accepts the outcome with grace. Though a home is sanctified by a believer's presence, Paul made it clear that one partner's salvation does not guarantee that the other will follow. Salvation is not ours to grant; each person must respond in faith to God's grace by their own volition.

In verse 16, Paul describes the believer as "not enslaved" or not "bound" to the marriage when the unbeliever leaves. Romans 7 talks about how a woman is "bound" by the law of marriage. It compares this to being bound by the law, enslaved to sin. When we die to the law, we are free from that which bound us, free to serve the new way of the Spirit. Just so, a believer is not bound to a marriage that the unbeliever leaves. The believer is freed from the marriage just as if the spouse had died. Though every attempt ought to be made toward reconciliation, it is clear that the believer may not be able to save the marriage. In that case, the believer is absolutely free to remarry.

Paul is adding a second exception to the covenant of lifelong marriage established in the creation narratives and continued through every significant teaching in Scripture. Jesus added an exception because of adultery and now Paul, inspired by the Spirit of Christ, adds an exception based on abandonment by an unbelieving spouse. Both exceptions are part of what Jesus spoke of concerning the hardness of heart of sinful mankind. In a perfect world, such exceptions would not be necessary, but this is a broken world. When one party's hard-hearted sin breaks a marriage covenant, the other party is not required to keep a covenant that has been shattered beyond repair. Marriage requires fidelity and it requires presence. When a spouse breaks the bond of fidelity, it threatens the core of the marriage. When the spouse leaves, the marriage covenant is broken. It takes two people to have a marriage covenant.

The second significant conclusion from this passage, which has been true throughout the Bible's teachings, is that a biblically approved divorce implies the right to remarry. Death ends the marriage – the only way God intended. But in the sinful world, a divorce based on the exceptions God has granted also ends the marriage and frees the innocent party to seek a new marriage relationship. The believer is no longer bound by the covenant of marriage because it has been broken by the other party. This will be significant in our discussion of ministry. A man who has been divorced on biblical grounds and is remarried can still be qualified as the "husband of one wife." The first marriage was broken by sin and he was granted peace and freedom by the Scriptures. In God's eyes, he has only one wife.

Remarriage is assumed in passages that deal with divorce. If a divorce is granted on biblical grounds, the marriage is over and the covenant is broken. The right to remarry is limited in Deuteronomy 24 (a man cannot remarry his ex-wife if she has married another and divorced him), in the Gospels (unless adultery has broken the marriage, remarriage is sin), and here. In the separation situation Paul discussed, when a wife separates from her husband who is abusing his authority, he limits her right to remarry. But these passages only make sense if they are limitations on an assumed right to remarry. A divorce that takes place based on biblical ground carries with it the right to seek a marriage – to a believer.

One more observation might be helpful here. Universal and strict rules and policies about divorce and remarriage are fraught with peril, often going beyond what the Bible says. There are basic principles taught in God's word that should not be ignored, but generally these do not lend to a simple list of policies. They require a case-by-case review. Developing a "one-size-fits-all" divorce policy while remaining biblical is a herculean task.

The believer's first responsibility in marriage is to walk in the power of God and seek to make the marriage work. We are not to look for the escape hatch, but to be marriage builders and agents of healing. We must forgive and seek restoration no matter how broken a marriage seems to be, remembering that our Savior make the lame walk, the blind see, and raised the dead. He has the power to heal our marriages as well.

A wife, who is called by God to live in submission to her husband, is given an option not granted to her husband. If he abuses his authority and creates a hostile environment for the marriage, she may separate from him and live as a single woman, out from under his authority. She has two options in this case. She may work through the problems and seek restoration with her husband, or she will have to live as a single woman the rest of her life. This is a separation and not a biblically-qualified divorce.

Finally, Paul adds a second exception to the biblical ideal of the lifelong covenant of marriage. As adultery can break the marriage covenant so also does abandonment by the unbelieving spouse. In this case, the believing spouse is free to live at peace, not bound to the covenant he or she made, and may seek a new marriage – all under the blessing of God.

A Theory

The obvious question is whether the principle in 1 Corinthians 7 ought to be applied strictly or whether it can be applied more broadly to other situations. Paul addressed the situations that existed in Corinth but are there situations that spring up in which the principles taught here can apply beyond the strict application of this passage? What if the one who leaves is a professing Christian (but is obviously not acting like one)? Are there other situations that might exist?

There is a clear progress in the biblical revelation on marriage and divorce issues in Scripture. In Deuteronomy, the absolute right of men to divorce their wives without cause was limited. In the Gospels, Jesus told men they couldn't divorce their wives unless there was adultery. In 1 Corinthians both men and women are given the right to divorce (and women the right to separate). The biblical teaching on the roles of men and women progresses throughout Scripture to its full New Testament revelation. Some have taken that a step further and argued what is sometimes called trajectory hermeneutics, that the trajectory of the biblical writers should be continued after the closing of the canon. They justify going beyond the teachings of Scripture into egalitarian views by arguing that the trajectory of Scriptures headed in that direction. Since the Bible moves towards a greater freedom and dignity for women, teachings such as wives submitting to their husbands, restrictions of leadership positions in churches to men, and other such teachings should be nullified. We cannot extrapolate from progressive revelation to justify our own ideas through trajectory hermeneutics. Though the word of God reveals its full truth gradually, that truth is consistent throughout. No truth taught in the Old Testament is nullified in the New Testament, only expanded. We cannot use the trajectory of Scripture to nullify the consistent teachings of Scripture.

Though we reject such trajectory interpretation and desire to hold to the biblical teaching, applying these principles to specific situations can be troublesome. The question remains, can we expand these principles beyond the narrow focus of 1 Corinthians 7? If a woman came to me, abandoned by her "Christian" husband, I would likely apply this teaching and advise her to accept the freedom of Christ. A man who names Christ but does not act like Christ – what are we to think? Anyone who is in ministry today knows that we face mind-boggling life-situations on a regular basis. What do we do? We study God's word and do the best we can to apply biblical principles to broken lives in a world that is so bizarre it makes that process difficult. We take the biblical principles and apply them as faithfully as we can in a sin-broken world.

A Christian who honors God and wants to please him will do everything he or she can to preserve the marriage. A godly person never looks for an excuse or justification for divorce but looks for ways to show love and seek the transforming power of God. Such a person would only take the divorce exceptions as a last resort, never an easy way out.

What Happens before Christ, Stays before Christ - 1 Corinthians 7:17-24

These verses establish an important principle. A person should remain in the marital position he or she was in at the point of salvation. In other words, salvation is a washing away of the past and implies a new, fresh start. All past sin is forgiven and the person is given a second (or third, or fourth) chance by God.

Paul tells believers in verse 24 that "In whatever condition each was called, there let him remain with God." Were you married? Seek to make the marriage work. Divorced and remarried? Accept God's forgiveness and the fresh start of grace. This principle probably also applies to polygamy, though that is not a significant issue in America. Of course, in this wicked world we will have some genuine challenges applying this principle, but a simple conclusion can be reached for our purposes in this book.

Paul is telling us that what happens prior to salvation should not be held against that person after salvation. How can someone who is enslaved to sin he held liable for sinning? Divorce that occurs pre-conversion should not be held against a person once they have been redeemed.

Summary

1. For Paul, divorce is not a first option, but a last resort. He affirms the teaches of the Genesis and of the Gospels that establish marriage as a lifelong covenant. However, as Jesus admitted an exception based on adultery, Paul added one based on abandonment by an unsaved spouse. A divorce on these grounds implies the right to remarry.

2. Husbands, given authority in their homes, are never allowed to initiate divorce or separation. They are to mimic the unconditional love of God and seek to rebuild the marriage.

3. Wives, living under their husbands' authority, are permitted to separate from unbelieving husbands who abuse them or create a cruel, hostile atmosphere in the home. She may live as a single woman or seek reconciliation with her husband, but this is not a divorce and she may not remarry.

4. Paul advanced the teaching of Jesus that the hardness of the human heart created a broken world in which God's ideal is sometimes impossible. The desire of every Christian ought to be to make marriage work, to seek healing and reconciliation. But when a marriage is broken

by the other party's infidelity or abandonment, the believer can live in peace and freedom, not bound by a marriage covenant the other has broken.

The devil is in the details, of course, and in this study, the hard part is application. What about this circumstance or that. Pastors must seek to faithfully apply God's word to people's lives, both calling sin sin and not heaping condemnation on those who are not sinning! Too often we have either excused what God condemns or condemned what God approves. We must walk the tightrope of grace and truth – a thing that will never be easy. But as shepherds of God's people, that is our duty.

Chapter 6: What Do We Say about Abuse?

"Go home and submit to your husband."

So much pain and hurt has been caused because pastors and church leaders have told women that they should submit to their abusive husbands. It is never easy to have a reasoned, biblical discussion of this subject because passions run so high. For some, anything short of "If a man hits you, divorce his sorry self," is an invitation to abuse and mistreatment. For others, such a position undermines the sanctity of marriage and God's design for the home. But The question we must ask is simple. What does God say? What does the word tell us on the topic? We must trust God and his word. Whatever it tells us on any subject will be true, it will be right, and it will be best. Obedience to God's word is the smartest strategy in any situation.

But what does God's word say? Strip away the emotion, the anger, the worldly viewpoints, and the question remains. Does abuse – verbal, physical, or sexual – constitute a biblical grounds for divorce? Or does the Bible support the advice of pastors and counselors who have told women to submit to their husbands, even those who are abusive?

Thinking Biblically about Abuse

Let me state something very clearly, before the discussion begins. Abuse of a woman by a man is despicable and inexcusable. When God gives someone authority, it must be used in the service of others, according to Christ's example. He is Lord of all, yet he came to serve and to give his life as a ransom for many. One who abuses the authority that God has given him to oppress, belittle, or hurt his wife or his children offends God. Husbands are to love their wives and seek to be a blessing to them. They are to nurture their children and not to damage them through cruelty and selfishness. Too many men have asserted their authority at home in ungodly ways, throwing their weight around, demanding to be served instead of serving, and seeking to control their families, even using abuse to do so. Many justify this using Scripture, but this evidences no understanding of biblical leadership and authority. That is not what God intended.

Unfortunately, abuse has become epidemic, even in Christian homes and in churches. It is hard to know how much of the increase in our knowledge of abuse results from increasing incidence of the sin and how much just has to do with reporting. Certainly, men have always abused their wives and parents have always been abusive to their children. We are, thankfully, less likely to sweep it under the rug today than we used to be. Churches are learning that hiding abuse is as wicked as the abuse itself.

However, in discussions of this topic, especially on my blog, I have noticed that reason seems to take flight when we turn our attention to abuse. I have read comments by Christian women who said that in this instance, we need to set the Bible aside because women who have been abused cannot be expected to do what the Bible commands. No! God's word is true for everyone. It is true in good times and in the worst of times. It is true even for those who have been abused.

Many unbiblical statements are made about those who abuse. Chief among them is the commonly held idea, "once an abuser, always an abuser." Yes, too many women have taken back a man who expressed remorse about his abuse, only to have him repeat his sin the next time he got angry. An abusive man (or woman) has become that due to deeply engrained sin and patterns of behavior. It will never be easy to change for one who abuses a woman or her children, but the Bible says, *"If anyone is in Christ he is a new creation. The old has gone; the new has come."* It does not say "If anyone but abusers are in Christ..." If anyone! No exceptions. Jesus changes lives. It may take time. A woman who has been abused should not believe that just because her husband says, "I prayed for forgiveness" that he is magically changed. If we deny the ability of an abuser to change, we are doing something far more sinister than denying the power of that sinner to change. We are denying the power of the Cross, the power of Christ to make sinners new. If Christ cannot change that sinner, what makes you think he can change you? Christ makes us new. He forgives, renews, rebuilds. Never lose sight of the transformational power of Christ.

However, it is equally unbiblical to simply tell a woman to go home and suffer abuse. Too many preachers, elders, deacons, and other church leaders have failed to understand the Bible's teaching on this topic and have sent women into dangerous situations where they suffered horribly. Jesus said that God knew the hardness of man's heart and allowed a divorce exception in the case of adultery. Because he knew the hardness of man's heart, he also provided a way for women whose husbands abuse their authority and treat them abusively to protect themselves and their children.

Perspectives

A few words of warning are in order as we approach this discussion. First, we will not waste time wondering if the abuse of a woman or children is ever justified. It is not. It is sinful and despicable, an offense against God. Men, you are leaders in your home, called to serve and bless your family, not to use and abuse them. There is nothing a woman does or can do that excuses your abuse – physical, sexual, or verbal – or makes it anything less than despicable.

When we are confronted with situations of abuse, our flesh tends to kick in. "Leave the jerk and go find someone who will treat you right so you can be happy." (Your instinct might be to substitute a stronger work for "jerk" but that's as strong as I go.) We want to tell someone who is abused that they are free to leave the abuser and find someone who will treat them in a better way. That is understandable, but we do not do biblical exegesis based on what we want or on what makes people feel good. Our goal is to please God and to live in obedience to him. We assume that what God says is right is also best. No matter how strongly I feel about something, it is not about my feelings, but about what the Bible says. I must study God's word and be guided by sound interpretation, not by my feelings, my anger, or my love for someone who has been injured. It is about God's word, not my feelings.

Our personal experiences are never a safe guide to biblical interpretation. Name a form of abuse and there is someone in my extended family or among my friends who has suffered it. Talking about abuse can get me emotional. Angry. Disgusted. Frustrated. I have had to deal with some horrific situations in counseling. Still, our duty is to exegete the word and interpret our feelings by what it teaches. We must not fit the word into our feelings. Of course, we all agree with this in theory, but on an emotional topic such as this it becomes difficult to hold the line.

I believe that the biblical pattern that we established earlier provides a framework that we can use to counsel the abused with wisdom, grace, and compassion. We can give them protection and still counsel obedience to God's word.

The Biblical Principles

Scripture gives two key teachings about marriage and divorce. First, God intended marriage to be a lifelong covenant. Since he put Adam to sleep and brought Eve into existence, that has been God's intent and it will continue to be so until the final trumpet blows. But Jesus taught us that sinfulness in the human heart motivated the introduction of exceptions to that lifelong covenant principle. In the gospels, Jesus gave one exception, adultery. Paul added another in 1 Corinthians 7, abandonment. These acts of sin break the marriage covenant.

In 1 Corinthians 7:10-11, we examined another set of circumstances in which Paul gave women an option which he did not extend to men, the option to separate from but not to divorce their husbands. Read the passage again.

To the married I give this command—not I, but the Lord—a wife is not to leave her husband. [11] But if she does leave, she must remain unmarried or be reconciled to her husband—and a husband is not to divorce his wife.

Husbands are not permitted to divorce their wives, but outside the boundaries of the exceptions given elsewhere – adultery and abandonment – a wife is permitted to separate from her husband. This is clearly not a divorce. She cannot remarry but must either live as a single woman or reconcile to her husband. Those are the facts, but they engender many questions.

First, why would Paul give an option to women that he does not give to men? Paul assigns different roles in marriage to men and women, based on the created order, the way God made us. Men have been given leadership in their homes, authority meant to be used for the blessing and benefit of those who live under it. Wives are commanded to submit to their husbands as unto the Lord in both Ephesians 5 and Colossians 3. Because she lives under her husband's authority, the wife is given an escape clause in verses 10 and 11. The man, given leadership by God, sets the tone in his home and is given no right to walk away, to separate from his wife. But a woman whose husband abuses his authority, who creates a hostile atmosphere in the home, is given the freedom to live separately as a single woman. Perhaps that action will motivate real change in her husband and she can reconcile or perhaps she will live single the rest of her life. But she is permitted to leave an intolerable marriage to live as a single woman.

Under what circumstances can a woman invoke that privilege? That answer would seem to flow from the first question. If a man uses his God-given authority to oppress or abuse his wife, or his children, to the extent that she finds living in that home intolerable, she is free in Christ to leave the home and live as a single woman.

Again, this is not a divorce. The marriage is not ended and she is not free to engage in new relationships. She can live by herself or she can renew her relationship with her husband, if she chooses. The covenant is suspended, not ended.

The important lesson here is that women are not required to endure abuse, cruelty, and other horrors to walk in obedience to Christ. Those pastors who have sent bruised and battered women back to their abusers have done so without biblical warrant. A high view of Scripture and of marriage does not require us to aid and abet abusers. That bit of bad advice needs to be replaced with a balance, biblical viewpoint.

I realize that most today counsel abused women that such abuse ends their marriage and they should move on. Divorce him and start over. I understand that impulse but I cannot find the justification for that in Scripture. I am bound by what I believe the Scripture says and I believe that for all of us, doing what God's word commands is best. I cannot give a "thus saith the Lord" to this view. It is my best interpretation of the biblical evidence and so I stand here until someone convinces me that the Bible teaches something else. Our authority is God's word, not our feelings, desires, or anger.

Biblical Perspectives on Abuse

1) We have no right to add a third grounds for divorce when the Bible does not.

The Bible gives two reasons for divorce; adultery and abandonment. Many have added a third ground for divorce, abuse. But we are on shaky ground when we allow our wisdom to replace that of the writers of Scripture and the Spirit who inspired the text. We cannot accept the lie that we have attained a moral superiority over the biblical writers – as though we know more and have better insight on these matters than those backward patriarchal Hebrews! That is both arrogant and heretical, an insult to the perfect word of God. We must not go beyond the word. There are two biblical grounds for divorce, not three.

2) We must not abuse the biblical teaching on authority to demand that women stay in abusive homes.

This must stop! Pastors must no longer tell abused women that God expects them to place themselves and their children in harm's way. We must not side with the abusers but must stand with the victims. Battered wives and victimized children must not be sent back to the homes where they have been hurt so that they can be harmed again. God forgive us for how we have damaged women and children with this unbiblical teaching. 1 Corinthians 7:10-11 is God's gift of protection to women whose husbands abuse the authority he gave them. Women are not commanded to submit to cruelty and abuse, and we must stop telling them that they are!

3) A woman who separates from her abusive husband has two biblical options.

She may decide that living single is better than living with her husband. Or, perhaps, if her husband goes through genuine repentance and spiritual transformation, she will return to him. That's it. She is not free to seek another man. She is separated, not divorced.

4) If an abused woman separates from her husband on these grounds, the church should support, encourage and help her, not judge her.

Too often, women have experienced judgment from the church when they have made known accusations of abuse. It grieves me to hear women tell of the shame and rejection they have experienced in churches after they have exposed their abusive husbands. The church ought to help abused women in every way they can, surrounding them with love, acceptance, and support. Don't circle the wagons around the husband but call him to repentance and draw the circle of support around the woman and the children who have been abused.

5) The same principles apply when a child is the one being abused.

No woman should stay in a home in which her child is endangered by an abusive man. It is fundamental to a woman's nature to protect her children. It would be despicable to suggest she should leave her children in danger. The principles of 1 Corinthians 7:10-11 would apply here.

6) To deny that abusive men can change is to deny Christ's power.

The idea that is commonly held in the world, "once an abuser, always an abuser," is even advocated by some in the church. Obviously, when someone abuses a woman or child, they are contemptible and deserve to be held to account by the law and the church. But we believe that Jesus changes lives, and that has to mean that he can change the heart of an abuser, even one who abuses children.

A woman who has been abused (or especially one whose children have been abused) should return to her husband because he says he's sorry and promises to change. But neither should she assume he can never change. God changes lives. He changes hearts. He transforms behavior.

It is right for a woman to demand that an abusive man give every evidence that his change is genuine before she believe him. There should be pastoral oversight and counseling as appropriate. But if we say that an abuser can never change, we are limiting the power of the Cross.

7) Abuse disqualifies a church leader.

It is amazing (and disgusting) that churches who will not even consider a man who has been divorced as a leader will allow those who abused women or children to continue in ministry. A man who abuses a woman or a child lacks the character to lead the people of God and there should be no question concerning this. It does not matter if the abuse is physical, sexual, or even verbal, a man who abuses God's sheep cannot be trusted as a shepherd.

Abusers cannot be leaders and leaders must not abuse.

Conclusion

So...

The church has too often given more support to the abuser than to the abused. That should not be. When a woman is abused, she should receive sound biblical advice and support from the church as she goes through the horrible challenge. But we must apply the teachings of the Bible even to difficult situations such as abuse. We cannot simply give permission the Bible doesn't or substitute our feelings for its teachings. The Bible gives a path for abused women to follow, and we should encourage them to follow it.

Chapter 7: Summary of Biblical Teachings on Divorce

There is both remarkable consistency and a clear progression in the biblical teaching on divorce. The cornerstone was set in Genesis 2:24 and then the foundation laid in Deuteronomy 24:1-4. Jesus erected the structure on that foundation in the Gospels (Matthew 10:3-12, Mark 10:2-12, Luke 16:18) and then Paul finished the building in 1 Corinthians 7. There are two basic principles that are established, interwoven, and fleshed out throughout these teachings. God intended for marriage to be a lifelong covenant but he also recognized that we live in a world broken by sin. In such a broken world the ideal sometimes becomes impossible. If one party to the covenant breaks it, the other cannot be bound by it. The principles are consistent in all the teachings, progressively developed to their full treatment in 1 Corinthians 7.

Our purpose in this study is to deal with the question of whether a man who has been divorced (or is married to a divorced woman) is disqualified from service as a pastor, elder or deacon according to God's word. That question can only be answered against the background of a clear understanding of the Bible's teachings on divorce and remarriage. If divorce is always sin and remarriage is always adultery, then divorced and remarried men are not likely qualified to serve in leadership roles. That is what the prohibitionist position has held through the years, the dominant position in evangelical churches. But that is not what the Bible teaches. The biblical position is much more nuanced. Divorce is not what God intends, but in a broken world it is what happens at times.

Before we engage the thorny issues of divorce, remarriage and ministry, let us briefly review the teachings we have established in this study. .

1. God intended marriage to be a lifelong covenant. This was the divine ideal from the beginning of time, clear from the Creation accounts in Genesis. God created us male and female and designed us to share a life together – one man and one woman commitment in a lifelong covenant, which would provide pleasure, blessing and companionship from both. Divorce was never part of God's pre-fall plan and it should not be viewed as an easy option when a marriage gets tough.

The problem with a study such as this is the danger of communicating a false message. We tend toward the extremes. On one extreme is the prohibitionist who says more than the Bible says, failing to recognize the reality of a broken world. But the reaction to that is often to become permissive. You aren't happy in your marriage? Don't worry! God forgives. Get a divorce and start over. God will give you a fresh start! NO! NO! NO!

We must walk that fine line, as difficult as it is, by always maintaining the biblical ideal of a lifelong joyous covenant. We must remember that God is there to help us, to empower us so that our marriages can be all that he wants them to be. We are not on our own.

And even when we have failed in our marriages the forgiveness he gives us can be extended to one another and destroyed marriages can be healed to the glory of God.

It is always to the greater glory of God to seek healing and restoration rather than divorce.

2. In a broken world, God makes provision for human sinfulness. Sin breaks us and it mars the beauty of what God created. The intent of God for marriage, a lifelong and joyous covenant, has been defaced by human sin, by infidelity, self-centeredness, and other perversions of what God intended. While some theological systems make no allowance for this, God's word does. "Because of the hardness of your hearts," Jesus said. God established exceptions to the lifelong marriage principle based on the sinful hardness of the human heart.

Divorce is never the first choice for a believer, but when a sinful partner in the marriage covenant irretrievably breaks the bond and is unwilling to work to heal it, the believer is not bound to that covenant. A marriage requires a husband and a wife. One person can't make it work. God understands this and provides grounds on which a marriage covenant can be recognized as broken.

3. The New Testament specifies two grounds for divorce. Jesus, building on Moses' teaching in Deuteronomy, established adultery as a grounds for divorce. The sexual bond is meant to be for a husband and wife alone, a sacred tie uniting them into one body. Paul, in 1 Corinthians 6, tells how serious a sin sexual immorality is. Jesus, in Matthew 19, allows that an unrepentant adulterous lifestyle breaks the marriage covenant and provides a grounds for the dissolution of a marriage.

In 1 Corinthians 7, Paul, dealing with a situation not previously extant, added a new exception. If an unbelieving spouse leaves a marriage, the believing spouse is not bound. Physical presence is essential to a marriage. If one partner leaves, the other cannot continue the marriage by himself or herself. That abandonment dissolves the marriage.

The exceptions actually prove the sanctity and importance of marriage. A husband and wife join together in a covenant before God. The covenant is based on promises and commitments made by both parties to the covenant. Husband and wife agree to be absolutely faithful to one another and to reject all sexual immorality. And they become one flesh, joined together not only physically, but emotionally, psychically, and spiritually. When one member breaks this covenant by a lifestyle of unrepentant sexual immorality or by abandoning his or her spouse, this breaks this holy bond. It is no small sin to break the bond of marriage, but God recognizes that when one partner voids the covenant, the other is released from it.

4. The Grounds for Separation – Paul, in recognition of the authority the husband has in the marriage, and the tendency of some husbands to abuse that authority, gives to the believing wife the right separate from her husband and live as a single woman or to seek reconciliation with her husband (1 Corinthians 7:10-11). Women who separate from their husbands on the grounds that he is impossible to live with, that he is abusive of his authority or that he treats her unkindly, have no right to remarry. This same right of separation is not granted to a husband, who has the authority and responsibility to demonstrate the proactive love of God and lead his home in the right ways.

5. Remarriage is assumed when a divorce is granted. From the Old Testament teachings to the teachings of Jesus through the final revelation to Paul, the assumption is that a biblical divorce ends a marriage and brings the right to remarry. That was established in the

Old Testament teaching and never countermanded. Jesus restricted remarriage except when the adultery exception was in place. What does that imply? When a divorce is biblically justified remarriage is assumed. Paul, in 1 Corinthians 7, distinguishes between the divorce exception in the event of abandonment and the simple separation privilege given to the wife. She cannot remarry. Why would that be established? Because remarriage is assumed in the case of a biblical divorce.

6. It's all about balance.

The truth in this teaching does not lie with the extremes – absolute prohibition or permissiveness. It is nuanced, and must be established on a case by case basis. Blanket policies are destined to be either hyper-biblical or unbiblical – to go beyond biblical standards or to go beyond them. Our duty is remember that those who struggle with their marriages need biblically accurate, gospel-focused, redemptive ministry, not platitudes, judgment and certainly not rejection or isolation.

The Finished Product

Applying the Biblical Principles of Divorce, Remarriage, and Ministry to Real-Life Church Situations

And overseer must be above reproach, the husband of one wife. 1 Timothy 3:2

Chapter 8: Husband of One Wife?

"I want to stick to the biblical standard. I don't think we should compromise the Bible to let divorced men serve as deacons."

That was the phrase my dear deacon friend spoke that has stuck with me all these years. He assumed, as many thousands, likely millions have, that the Bible required that divorced men be excluded from service as pastors, elders, or deacons. This came from a heart of fidelity to God's word, a sense that to do anything else would be to give in to the spirit of the world, to compromise truth. I have tried to establish in this book that that Bible's teaching does not support the prohibitionist position as many have assumed it does. Now, we turn our attention to the focus of this book. What about pastors? What about elders? What about deacons? Are divorced men eligible to serve in these positions? Are men married to divorced women eligible to serve?

One (Not So) Simple Phrase

The crux of the issue is one small phrase that appears twice in 1 Timothy 3 (verse 2 concerning "overseers" (pastors/elders) and in verse 12 concerning deacons) and again in Titus 1:6 as a requirement for elders. Elders and deacons were both required to be "the husband of one wife." That is the sum total of the biblical evidence. The prohibitionist says that phrase means (or at least includes the concept) "never divorced" and eliminates anyone who has ever been divorced and remarried. I maintain that it does not mean that, that it has a different meaning and is not focused primarily on divorce. It goes far beyond that. I hope to demonstrate that theory convincingly and show that this phrase has a much more powerful meaning than we've previously assigned to it.

So, what is "a husband of one wife?" Answers to this question have generally fallen into three broad categories, though many theories have been presented. The easiest explanation is that this is a prohibition against polygamy and the primary focus was monogamy. The second is that favored by prohibitionists, the idea that the phrase is synonymous with "never divorced" and is a simple prohibition of those who have been divorced and remarried serving as church leaders. The third view, which I hold, focuses more on marital fidelity and devotion, being a "one-woman man."

What does the phrase mean? One of the chief battles in theological argument is the "burden of proof" battle. Each side wants to hold the middle and shift the burden to the other side to prove their point. I would challenge the prohibitionist to prove that the phrase really does mean what they say it means and they would argue that it is up to me to prove that it does not. The fact is that we all bear the burden of proof. The Bible puts the burden on both sides of arguments like this. In Revelation 2, Jesus rebuked Pergamum and Thyatira for tolerating sin. We should never tolerate what God has called a sin. If the prohibitionists are right, we are sinful to tolerate divorced leaders in the church, no matter what our culture says. On the other hand, Paul repeatedly warns against human rules. In 1 Corinthians 4:6 he commands the people not to "go beyond what is written." Galatians and Colossians both carry similar warnings. If "husband of one wife" does not mean never divorced, we must stop disqualifying from leadership those whom God has not disqualified.

In Revelation 22:18-19, John gives this warning about the prophecies he has written. "*I warn everyone who hears the words of the prophecy of this book: if anyone adds to them, God will add to him the plagues described in this book, and if anyone takes away from the words of the book of this prophecy, God will take away his share in the tree of life and in the holy city, which are described in this book.*" Severe penalties attach to either adding to or taking away from the words of the prophecy. Perhaps that warning is specific to the Revelation, but the principle is instructive for us.

It would be deeply damaging to the Body of Christ to allow divorced men to serve in leadership positions if the Scriptures prohibit it. But it would be just as serious a sin to prevent men from serving without biblical warrant. It is not acceptable to either take away from the teachings of scripture or to add to them. The burden of proof rests on all of us. We must go to God's word and be guided by its teachings.

So, what is "the husband of one wife?"

Husband of One Wife - Possibilities

Let's examine the various views on the meaning of this phrase.

1) Polygamy.

Many have taken this in the most literal sense possible, as a condemnation of polygamy. The common English translation of the phrase would seem to differentiate the husband of one wife from the husband of more than one wife. It is the simplest and most literal interpretation.

But two objections can be raised to cast doubt that this phrase speaks of polygamy. First, there is scant evidence of widespread polygamy in Roman culture. By this time, it was limited among the Jews, but not absent. Polygamy was present but not enough that Paul would likely have made it a point of leadership in a letter to churches in a Greek or Roman culture.

But the most devastating evidence against the polygamy interpretation is found in 1 Timothy 5:9, where the same phrase is used with the gender roles reversed. Widows who were going to be added to "the list" (we know little about that list) had to have been "the wife of one husband." Regardless of how common polygamy (more than one wife) was, polyandry (a wife with more than one husband) is among the rarest of cultural phenomena. Paul would not have bothered, in patriarchal cultures, to restrict women who had more than one husband when no women had more than one husband. The fact that the identical phrase is used to describe men makes it unlikely that polygamy is the focus there either.

Polygamy was not part of God's plan and in cultures where it is practice, this passage would apply. But Paul had more in mind here than a simply prohibition on polygamy. Men with multiple wives should not be in leadership positions in the church, but that is not the primary intent of this passage.

2) Never divorced.

Commonly, this verse has been used as a proof text for the prohibition of divorced men serving in leadership roles in the church. The logic is actually derived from the polygamy argument. Jesus said that those who divorced on grounds other than adultery and remarried were committing adultery. Essentially, they were married to two women. A divorced man (or a man married to a divorced woman) is a spiritual polygamist. He is married to both his current wife and, in the eyes of God, the wife he divorced.

There is no monolithic uniformity in the prohibitionist group. Some apply the prohibition to all who are divorced. Others grant grace to those whose divorces took place before conversion. How can we hold someone accountable for their actions before their conversion? Other variations occur. But the core of the position is that "husband of one wife" could essentially be translated as "never divorced." I would argue that there is a clearer way that Paul could have said that if that were his intent.

3) Marital fidelity and devotion

The third view, the one I hold, is that this passage does not refer to divorce or polygamy, but to the kind of husband a man is to his wife. A better translation may be, "a one-woman man." Am I a devoted and faithful husband, giving myself body, soul, and spirit to my wife to bless her and to meet her needs? This interpretation goes far beyond the question, "Have I avoided sleeping with other women?" I can state categorically that in my 37 years of marriage (and the nearly 21 years of my life before that) I never committed adultery a single time. Not once. But have I always been a faithful, devoted, selfless, Christlike husband? Yikes! That is a much tougher standard, one I fail continually.

I am discounting the polygamy view, but before I give focus to the pros and cons of the "Never divorced" and "Faithfulness" views, it would be helpful to dig into the text.

Exegesis – What Does "Husband of One Wife" Mean? ,

It is my contention that neither divorce nor polygamy is the primary focus of this passage, but that Paul is establishing faithfulness and devotion as the standard of a godly leader. Those who lead others in God's church much be examples to God's people of what a husband ought to be. What does the text say?

The translation "husband of one wife" is not the best translation of the passage. The Greek phrase in 1 Timothy 3:2, "mias gunaikos andra," could be literally translated "one-woman man" or "a man of one woman." A few verses later (verse 12), Paul uses an identical phrase, except that the last word, "man" is plural instead of singular. In Titus 1:6 Paul uses a nearly identical form of the phrase from verse 2, except that he uses a slightly different word for "man" – synonymous and without a significant difference. The elders and overseers of the church (what we often call pastors) and the deacons were to be "one-woman men," the best translation of that phrase.

That translation seems to explain itself, as does a biblical view of leadership. A godly leader has a much higher calling than to simply limit himself to sexual relations with one woman only. I could spend my entire life sleeping with one woman but ignore her needs, treat her dismissively, prioritize everything else above her. I may never divorce her or commit adultery against her, but I do not fulfill the biblical demand to be a "one-woman man." God calls me to faithful and devoted, to serve my wife's needs. If I do not properly serve my wife and my family, how can I be trusted to serve the church? If I treat my wife selfishly, using her to meet my needs and ignoring hers, will I not be likely to do the same when I lead the church of God? The demands of ministry are difficult, and if I have not managed my household well and served my family, especially my wife, faithfully, how can I be expected to serve well as a leader in the church? My devotion to my wife and my service to her is a test-case for my devotion and service to the Body of Christ.

Contrary to the accusations that are often made, this is not a lessening of the biblical standard, but it raises it dramatically. I can testify to my absolute sexual fidelity to my wife, before marriage and every day since. But have I met the "one-woman man" standard? I've struggled with that standard and often failed it.

That is the nature of leadership in the church and the way that our Savior works. He raises the bar, much as he did in Matthew 5, in the Sermon on the Mount. Leadership is about going beyond simple obedience to an external statute like, "marry one woman and only have sex with her." That is a good rule and a basic biblical standard. But for leadership in the church something much more difficult is demanded. I must do more than simply survive in marriage, but must devote myself as a husband to one woman, serving her and loving her, as Christ loved the church. If I want to lead the church, my heart must be faithful, not just my body. I must not be given over to pornography, to flirtation, to unhealthy relationships, and especially to ministerial mistress of pastoral success. I must be the husband of one wife.

There are ways that Paul could have said, "never divorced" if that was his intent. The Greek language has other constructions that would have communicated that more clearly. "Husband of one wife" has to do with heart and character not just with behavior. Men who lead the church of Jesus Christ must be devoted not only to the Savior, but to their wives, demonstrating their character and their ability to serve with fidelity in the church of Christ.

A Husband of One Wife – Definitions

So much hangs on one nebulous and disputed phrase. Perhaps the early Christians knew exactly what Paul meant by the phrase but unfortunately today, we do not. We tend to imbue it with the meanings we give it based on our views of divorce and remarriage. All of us condemn eisegesis but also engage in it at some level. But I will attempt to spell out as clearly as I can precisely what I think the word means. It is the sum-total of the Pauline marriage requirement for leaders. A pastor or elder, a deacon – he must be the husband of one wife. It is as simple as that. The tricky part is accurately defining that word. Here is what I believe it means.

1. A husband of one wife is, well, a husband with one wife.

I have assumed that the audience of this book would be an evangelical and largely complementarian group. I've not debated the women in ministry issue nor have I spent a lot of time on the issue of same sex marriage. But there seem to be at least three literal takeaways here about leadership in the church.

First, he must be a husband. This fits in with every other scriptural admonition on the topic that, while offending our modern egalitarian mores, restricts the role of pastor, elder, and even deacon (though there are some questions about the deacon ministry I don't have time to get into here) to men. This role is restricted to men.

Second, this passage would clearly rule out same sex marriages as appropriate for leadership in the church. It is hard to believe that I am actually writing this, and when I first penned this paper in seminary, this application never even would have crossed my mind. Even liberal churches did not ordain homosexuals back then. Now, though, even churches that self-identify (self-deceive?) as evangelical are performing same-sex marriages and considering homosexuals for clergy positions.

There is no way the husband of one husband or the wife of one wife could qualify for ministry under this Scriptural standard.

Finally, this passage clearly condemns the practice of polygamy. I have said that polygamy is not the primary focus and I stand by that. But it is condemned, nonetheless. Though God tolerated polygamy among his people in Old Testament days it was never part of his created plan and in the New Testament church he made that eminently plain. "We don't have polygamy in America," you say. Well, first of all, you are wrong about that. Secondly, just wait. If we tipped the first domino of gay marriage and told people you can love whomever you wish to love, can polygamy, polyandry, and all sorts of other perversions be far behind? The biblical standard will not change. One man. One woman.

So, just to get this out of the way, the literal application of this verse is clear. A leader in the church needs to be in a heterosexual monogamous marriage.

2. This does not exclude the single from leadership.

Some have argued that this limits leadership in the church to only those who are married. If a pastor, elder, or deacon is required to be the "husband of one wife" then a single man is not qualified to serve in that way, as he is clearly not a husband. In my pastorate in Cedar Rapids we had a lengthy discussion among the deacons about that as we were formulating our policies. It is a reasonable argument but I believe it is not correct.

The phrase is not designed to teach that a man must be a husband but to instruct the church on what kind of husband a man must be. It assumes that a man is a husband, as most men were. The choice to be single was not one that was made by many man in that era. I do not believe Paul was commanding marriage but was instructing husbands on how they were to treat their wives.

We must remember that the two most significant figures in the Christian church were single men. Some have argued that Paul had to have been married, because it was a requirement of Pharisees. Either he was a widow or a divorcee. But that is all conjecture. In all of his ministry he was a single man. As a matter of fact, he surrounded himself with a group of men and we know nothing about wives for Timothy, Titus, Aristarchus, Gaius, Luke or any of the men who were trained under Paul.

In fact, in 1 Corinthians 7, Paul said that if one could control his sexual desires, the single life was superior to the married life in many ways, because the single man could give himself fully to the work of the Lord. It is hard to see how Paul could say what he said in 1 Corinthians 7 and then turn around and restrict single men from serving as leaders in the church.

Single men are not disqualified from serving as leaders of the church under the "husband of one wife" qualification.

3. A husband of one wife is a faithful, loving, servant to his wife.

The essence of Christian leadership is service and sacrifice. In the kingdom of God, those with authority become servants of those they lead. The training ground for that leadership is the home. If a man treats his wife with disdain, if he ignores her needs and cares little for her feelings while he pursues his "ministry" he is not likely to be a faithful servant of the people of God.

During the Clinton scandals of the 1990s we were bombarded with the concept that a man could be a great leader while his private life was a mess. The Bible disagrees. Our public ministry flows from our private life. The way a man loves and leads his wife is both a model and a training ground for the way he will love and lead the people of God. If he is self-centered and unfaithful in one he will tend to be the same way in the other.

I have spent much time developing this concept already and will not reiterate all that has been said. I believe this is the heart and soul of what it means to be a "one-woman man." Is the way that a man loves, leads, and serves his wife an example to the church of how Christ loved the church? Is he a role model to the church? If he leads the church the way he leads his home, will the church prosper? That is what it means to be a "one-woman man."

4. A husband of one wife is not flirtatious or inappropriate with other women.

There is a lot of middle ground between faithful to my wife and adulterous. Two men can both say, "I've never cheated on my wife." But one is loving and devoted to his wife. The other constantly flirts with other women. He makes inappropriate comments. He eyes women every chance he gets. His imagination runs wild. He puts himself in intimate situations alone with other women. It never goes too far, but it goes far enough that he gets an ego boost from the adulation of that other woman.

There is an old song, "I only have eyes for you." In this visually stimulating world, that is a challenge. But a leader in a church needs to have a wife who is assured that her place in his heart and his life is not in any danger. She needs to be secure in his love, that she is a priority in his life. Perhaps our song needs to be, "I only have heart for you." My wife needs to know that when I speak to other women, my heart is hers, when I spend long hours at the church, my heart is hers.

5. A husband of one wife is not addicted to pornography.

Pornography is one of the biggest problems in marriages today. When I was a kid, it was out there but you had to go somewhere to find it. I wouldn't have known where to go. Now, you have to work hard to keep from being affected. Men often do not realize the damage that pornography does to women.

First of all, when you are using pornography, you are aiding and abetting in a small way or in a large way the human trafficking problem. We cannot decry the evil of that industry while clicking on porn. But the effect on our wives is terrible as well. How many of them can really match up to the surgically enhanced porn stars? If I love my wife, do I want to make her insecure and create feelings of inadequacy? I read one of those "eww" articles recently. It discussed some of the sexual practices that are common in porn. It (thankfully) didn't go into a lot of detail but much of what you see when you watch porn is nearly physically impossible unless you are a gymnast or a superhero. It creates an artificial, unreachable standard for women that few (none?) can meet. Also, the entirety of porn is about women pleasing men. It's fake. Women do not generally enjoy the things that men do to them in porn. So, when you are using porn, you find yourself wanting your wife to do things she likely can't do and she won't enjoy doing to fulfill a fantasy you created watching fictional sex on the internet. It is not loving at all. It destroys women's body-image and security and makes them feel cheap and used. Your wife is not a sex toy to be used for your pleasure.

We live in a despicable, dirty, sex-saturated and nasty world. Living clean in our world is more difficult than it has ever been. But a man of God, a "husband of one wife" must be an exemplary man who honors his wife in every way, including honoring the marriage bed.

107

6. A husband of one wife is imperfect.

No church should assume or expect that its pastor is perfect. The standards of 1 Timothy 3 and Titus 1 are not absolute or standards of perfection. If they were, I can promise you that the pulpit at my church would be empty. The standard is the ability to lead and to tell the people of the church, "Follow me." Pastors and deacons are men in the struggle as much as anyone else. But they must be men who have struggled and progressed to a point where they can help the rest of the church in its struggle.

7. Ultimately, the church must make a decision

At the final analysis, the church has to make a decision and then be responsible before God for that decision. Until we have the final clarity of glory we will have disagreements and will approach this in different ways. Two churches with pastors and who love God, love the word of God, study it diligently and seek to understand it, will come to different opinions on the issues related to divorce, remarriage and ministry. While I am convinced that the Scripture is on my side in this issue I admit that others have studied the same Bible and come to a very different conclusion. Different churches come to different opinions. We should accept that this universal agreement among faithful Christians is not possible on this issue.

The church must make these decisions. It cannot shirk the responsibility by trying set blanket policies that ignore that try to pretend that all divorces are created equal. There is no simple and fair template to apply to every situation that can keep the church from looking at the details and making those hard calls. We must walk that biblical tightrope; neither adding to nor taking away from the biblical revelation. Fortunately, we have the word of God and the Spirit to illumine us as we study it. Trust that God will give wisdom and guidance to the church that seeks him.

Conclusion

I am not deluded that my treatment will end debate on this topic, but perhaps we can at least all agree that at the heart and soul of Paul's instructions to Timothy and Titus is this – men who lead Christ's church need to be men of character, fidelity and commitment in marriage. They must be the kinds of husbands who are examples of Christlike service and love, proving they are ready to lead the Bride of Christ as they have led in their homes.

Chapter 9: Does Time Heal All Wounds?

Perhaps it is time to address the elephant in the room. What happens to the sinful party in a divorce? Is he forever disqualified from ministry leadership or does the grace of God eventually erase even his sin?

I am quite confident that the Scripture is clear (though many will disagree) on the basics of the biblical approach to divorce, remarriage, and ministry. This question, however, is not as easy for this author to answer. Some will jump to an immediate "yes" – these sinners can be forgiven but they are disqualified from leadership positions as long as they live. I remain conflicted about answering this question. It is rooted in two conflicting godly characteristics – God's glorious holiness and his amazing grace.

The question is not whether the blood of Christ can cover that sin. We must never ask that question about anyone. The blood has the power to cleanse the sin of adulterers, homosexuals, murderers, drug addicts, those who have had or encourage others to have abortions, abusers, child molesters, the worst third-world genocidal despot! – you name it, Christ can wash it away. If you deny the power of Christ to redeem any of those sinners, it is self-righteousness to believe he can redeem yours. The man who abandons his wife and children for another woman (or vice versa) can find forgiveness and spiritual restoration in Christ. He or she should also find forgiveness and fellowship in the church. A church that excludes or isolates repentant sinners is insulting the Savior's work at the cross and is mimicking the Pharisees more than the Savior. Jesus died for sinners and the church must celebrate those who repent. The blood of Christ cleanses and the church of Christ receives sinners.

But the question is whether such a sin permanently disqualifies a man from consideration for positions such as pastor, elder, or deacon. Does time vitiate the offense? Can a man who failed in a marriage, who divorced because of his own sin, and who remarried in violation of Scripture ever be considered eligible for service? Let's play pretend here. Imagine a man who 25 years ago walked out on his wife and children for a young woman he met at work. He pursued the woman, began the affair, divorced his wife, and married the younger woman. Guilty! A few years later he came to his senses and genuinely repented of his sin. He sought out his ex-wife and begged her forgiveness. He humbled himself before his children and let them know how ashamed he was of the sin he committed and the terrible example he gave to them. He went before his church to seek forgiveness as well. In the over twenty years since that repentance, he has been a godly man. He and his second wife have three children of their own who all love the Lord. He has a cordial relationship with his ex-wife and has rebuilt ties with his children from the first marriage. People know him as a man of God and in the business world his integrity and decency are beyond reproach. There is absolutely no question that he is qualified to be a deacon, elder or pastor on every other qualification in 1 Timothy 3 or Titus 1, but the memory of his heinous sin remains. Does it eliminate him? Does his sin from a quarter of a century ago negate all that God is doing in and through him today? Or does the man he has become in Christ nullify the sin of his past?

Competing Truths

The issues here are anything but simple as we balance two competing truths. We have already discussed the nature of the gospel and transforming power of Christ. Paul was an enemy of the gospel, a murderer, whom God made into a missionary. He was a prime example of the power of the gospel to save sinners. Peter denied Christ. Mark ran home crying to momma. God reclaims and restores the fallen. David was an adulterous murderer. The glory of God is seen in the worst of sinners becoming the best of servants of Christ.

Does divorce stand in a different category? If the sin in the scenario above were just about any other there would be no discussion. The sins of his ancient past would be considered under the blood and ancient history. He'd be asked to give testimony to the life-changing power of Christ at his ordination service! But divorce, because it involves the lifelong covenant of marriage, is placed in a different category. Forgiveness and restoration are granted (at least in theory), but the sin is a perpetual black mark which eliminates the man from leadership positions in the church as long as he lives.

Of course, marriage is the highest of commitments and failure in marriage reveals a deep character flaw that should not be ignored. It creates ongoing consequences and difficulties that affect leadership ability. And, of course, there are the words of Jesus that identify the second marriage as adultery. Does this mean that the second (or third) marriage is a continuing act of adultery? If so, then the remarried would be living in adultery and disqualified from leadership positions. Adulterers should not be pastors, elders or deacons. It that is what Jesus meant, the case is closed.

As we work through this, we will balance the grace of God with biblical standards of holiness and a respect for the sanctity of marriage. This is not as simple as some want to make it. We must fit the biblical evidence together to make a reasoned argument and ask whether such a man can ever again be qualified to lead the church.

Biblical Evidence

The primary concern in this discussion is what Jesus meant in the Gospel accounts when he said that the man who divorces and remarries commits adultery. He makes that statement in Matthew 5:32, Matthew 19:9, Mark 10:11-12, and Luke 16:18. In the Matthew passages, he includes the divorce exception, and there are a couple of minor variations. But the main teaching is consistent. A man who divorces, without adultery present, is committing adultery when he remarries. The question is what Jesus meant by that statement. Did the adultery take place when the man entered into the new marriage, or was Jesus claiming that the new marriage would be a continual act of adultery? Does the adultery last as long as the marriage lasts?

The primary evidence for the "perpetual adultery" view is the use of the present tense for "commit adultery" in all four passages. Back in the Medieval Era, when I was studying Greek, much was made of the "kind of action" of Greek verbs. The present tense was "continual action," an ongoing process. That Jesus used that tense in this warning was seen to imply that that adultery was perpetual as long as the marriage lasted. I am told, though, that Greek scholars are now saying that the emphasis on "kind of action" in my day was overblown. To ground our exegesis in the kind of action of Greek tenses is not recommended. So, the use of the present tense is not decisive as it was once assumed to be.

A contrary hint (and it is admittedly only a hint) comes from how Jesus designates the relationship after the unauthorized divorce. He refers to it as a marriage. The woman at the well was "married" five times, according to Jesus. This is not dispositive, but it is interesting. He does not negate the relationships but calls them marriages. These subsequent marriages were called marriages, not "affairs."

Argument from silence is always considered weak, but in this case it might be significant. Jesus, Paul, Peter, and the rest of the biblical authors took uncompromising stands against adultery. If adulterous relationships were ongoing in the church, Paul would not have hesitated to confront them and call the offenders to repentance. But none of the New Testament authors even called those involved in second (or third, or…) marriages to leave those marriages. If such a marriage were perpetual adultery, would not Paul or Peter or James call the church to confront such sin and discipline the sinner? I read (well, skimmed) a book that made this argument based on a letter by the church father Jerome. Why didn't Jesus or the Apostles make such an argument? Why did they not call the believer engaged in an adulterous second marriage to repent and leave the marriage for celibacy? Ezra did not hesitate to call Israel to leave their sinful marriages to the Canaanites, why would the New Testament authors not call the church to purify itself from such sin? The answer is simple. Entering such a marriage was viewed as an act of adultery, the breaking of the vows of the previous marriage. But entering the new marriage was an adulterous act that broke the covenant of the previous marriage. It was not perpetual adultery. It was the initiation of the marriage that was the sin.

In fact, if we argue that remarriage after divorce is perpetual adultery, it is silly to discuss whether leadership is an option. The question is why are these people are allowed to be members. The issue is not whether such a person should be a pastor, an elder, or a deacon, but whether church discipline should be put into effect. If a man is living in an ongoing adulterous relationship he should be called to repentance. The fact that this argument is never made in Scripture, that the remarried are never called to leave their "adulterous" marriages in repentance, is evidence that the sin Jesus intended to focus on was the initiation of a marriage when the previous marriage did not end on biblical grounds.

This is not to diminish the sin. If the divorce did not take place on biblical grounds, then remarriage is a sin, an act of defiance against God's will. It is sin and can only be corrected through repentance toward God and toward those people who have been offended by the sin. That sin will have consequences. When David committed adultery, he repented and was forgiven, but the consequences of that sin followed him and his family from that day forward. No Christian is wise to take sin lightly, or to think, "It's no big deal. I'll sin, then repent, and everything will be okay." Yes, God forgives. But the ripples of sin can go on and on in so many ways. Often it is our children and grandchildren who suffer the weight of that sin. Never ignore the commands of God or the importance of Jesus's words.

The biblical evidence is not beyond dispute. But it does not seem warranted to argue that remarriage after an unsanctioned divorce is perpetual adultery. The sin is entering into a marriage which breaks the sanctity of the marriage bond. Devastating consequences will result and the only solution is repentance and restitution.

Qualifying as a Leader

Once the sinner seeks forgiveness, can the disqualification brought by the infidelity ever be removed? Can such a man ever be qualified, or does his divorce disqualify him permanently? I love to be able to give definitive and clear answers from God's word, but it is my judgment that anyone who answers this question dogmatically is speaking with more confidence than the Scriptures warrant. There is no smoking gun here – it's a circumstantial case at best. I will lay out the evidence that I use to make my decision and then I will give my conclusions.

The Evidence

Note that in this discussion, we are addressing second (or third, or…) marriages in which the divorce did not take place according to biblical guidelines. When the divorce occurred because of adultery or abandonment, remarriage is not a sin – by the words of both Jesus and Paul. We are focused on marriages that ended when the biblical exceptions did not take place. What happens when a marriage ends for "irreconcilable differences?" Or what happens to the guilty party in an affair or the one who walks out and abandons his family? If we assume that later (too late to heal and restore the marriage) that person repents and returns to Christ, what is supposed to happen? How should the church respond?

1. It is the act of entering a second marriage that Jesus addressed. He was not attempting to define second marriages as perpetually adulterous. We have already reviewed the evidence on this and have admitted that it is not definitive. But the preponderance of the evidence leans toward the belief that initiating a marriage when the first marriage was still in place in God's eyes is the adulterous act. The second marriage breaks the marriage covenant and ends the frist marriage in sin. Even most prohibitionists reject the perpetual adultery position. It would require that the church not only exclude such people from leadership but also from membership.

The second marriage is a sin and it requires repentance before God, before the church, and before the wounded parties, but thereafter it is a marriage and it should be seen as a covenant before God.

2. The consequences of such an adulterous second (or third or more) marriage cannot be discounted. The truth in Scripture is usually found by balancing the extremes, not choosing between them. No, I do not believe in the concept of perpetual adultery and I certainly believe that those who repent will find that the blood of Christ cleanses from all sin – fully, completely, eternally, and radically. But this should not lead us to ignore the seriousness, even the ongoing seriousness, of such adulterous second marriages. Like David's sin, such adulterous second marriages will have pain attached.

I was counseling a man in an unhappy marriage. He had met a woman at work who was his "soulmate" and was planning to leave his wife to enter a relationship with the new woman. His words haunt me. "It's okay, Dave. I will confess the sin and God will forgive me." His flippant attitude toward sin and his intentional abuse of God's grace was horrifying. He completely ignored the concept of the consequences of his sin. In 2 Samuel 1-10, David experiences victory after victory. In chapter 11 we see the sad story of his fall into sin. Though he repents in chapter 12, the rest of the book records one devastating consequence after another in his family and in the nation he led. Affected his family and he lacked the moral authority to guide them. The nation rebelled and divided. David received grace but the people around him experienced great pain. His sin severely compromised his ability to lead the people.

Sin will be forgiven when we repent. That was guaranteed by the cross of Christ. But there will be pain and that pain can affect a man's ability to lead. A bitter ex-wife. A battered reputation. Broken or damaged relationships with children. The detritus of divorce cannot be discounted and is a significant factor in deciding whether someone is qualified to serve as a leader in the church.

3. No one is a natural Christian leader. The traits that qualify us are built by Christ over time. The character qualities of leaders in both 1 Timothy 3 and Titus 1 have to do with who the man is, not what he used to be. Leadership is about what a man has become, about how the Christ has worked in us and the fruit the Spirit has developed in us, not our natural personality traits. There is not a single one of the traits from Timothy and Titus that come naturally to me. They are qualities that God had to develop in me over time. As the Spirit has worked to make me more like Christ these qualities become more and more a part of my life (in theory, at least!).

There are two assumptions here. First, I was not always qualified as a leader. A person might have natural leadership qualities, but no one meets the standards of 1 Timothy 3 and Titus 1 in their natural state. The qualities there are supernatural, not natural. So, at some point, by the work of Christ within, I became qualified and ready to lead the church. I was not; now I am. Leadership is never about what I used to be but about what I have become in Christ. Do I have the character and godly reputation to inspire the church to follow me as

I follow Christ? It is what I am, what I have become, not what I used to be that is the issue.

But, when it comes to divorce, all the rules change. Every other quality in 1 Timothy 3 and Titus 1 is about what a man is, but we have made "one-woman man" (husband of one wife) about what a person was 10, 15, or 20 years ago. Why would one character quality be completely different from all others? As I have already argued, the best interpretation of "one-woman man" interprets it as a character quality – a man who demonstrates Christlike love and fidelity to his wife – not as a definer of the past, "never divorced." All the other qualities are focuses on a man's current character. We do not say, "this character quality must have been true of you all of your life." We say that it must be true now. I do not believe there is biblical warrant to treat divorce as a completely separate category of sin. It is about the kind of husband he is today.

Return to the scenario above. If the man had lived a life of promiscuity, had been a criminal, had committed any of a laundry list of other sins, we would rejoice that God had changed him and had made him new. Leadership in the church is about present character and not about past behavior. Does the fact that his sin was divorce differentiate it from all others?

So, the evidence here is nuanced. On the one hand we prize the grace of God and his renewal. On the other hand, we value the sanctity of marriage, recognize the initiation of a second marriage without a sanctioned divorce as sin, and acknowledge that consequences will come in due season. The church must walk the tightrope balancing these two values and in this question they come into direct conflict. How does the church deal with such a situation?

What Should a Church Do?

I am deeply conflicted about answering this for two reasons. First, I have carried on a long internal argument about where I believe the biblical evidence leads. My heart tells me that the gospel is about forgiveness and wiping away the sins of the past, about the transformational power of our Savior and giving people a fresh start. But my head also warns me that there are consequences to sins and we must not ignore that. Paul tells us that reputation to outsiders is a concern for leadership within the church, and an ugly divorce in a man's history could affect his ability to lead in the present. My second conflict has to do with the effect of this chapter on the readers. I have tried to balance the competing claims of the sanctity of marriage and the grace of God for sinners. I fear that this chapter will lead some to see me as ignoring biblical standards and discounting the importance of the lifelong covenant of marriage. I have tried to write this book balancing those claims and realize that this chapter may become a focal point of criticism for some.

Recognizing that, I am responsible to what I believe the word teaches, regardless of the consequences. Many factors go into making this decision and for me it is a split decision and a narrow one at that. Under the rarest and most limited of circumstances I believe that the grace of God could overcome the consequences of divorce, even one in which a man was at fault.

Divorce is still a big issue, perhaps the biggest. In most situations in which a man was at fault in his divorce, when he divorced his wife without biblical warrant, he is not qualified to be a leader in the church. But can such a man, over time, experience Christ's transformation, make restitution, rebuild his character, and develop the character, integrity and reputation necessary to lead the Body of

Christ? I believe he can. In most cases, it is best for him, for his family, and for the church, for such a man to serve God in non-leadership positions, but neither the words of Christ nor the Pauline qualifications in 1 Timothy or Titus would eliminate the possibility that he could return to some form of leadership. Lightning strikes. Sharks bite. And sometimes, such a man might be the man God would set forward for leading the church. It would be rare, perhaps more rare than lightning or shark bites, but I maintain that the possibility exists.

Considerations

1. Sin before conversion should be treated differently. Does it not seem absurd to disqualify a man from leadership because of something he did before he was saved? "If anyone is in Christ, he is a new creation…unless it was a divorce!" The blood of Christ washes away all sin. If someone can explain how eliminating a person from consideration from

Yes, even pre-conversion sins can have consequences. Salvation is not a get out of jail free card. There may be a bitter ex-spouse – a complicating factor for a church leader, to be sure. Issues with children – custody battles, yours-mine-ours difficulties – these can all complicate the work of a man in serving the church and may affect a church's decision on leadership. But to hold a man accountable for that which he did before Christ redeemed him and Spirit of God indwelled him is absurd.

2. The burden of proof is on the sinner. This is true of all of us. There is no right to leadership positions, they are earned by proving our maturity to our church family. When someone has committed a disqualifying sin, that burden grows heavier. He must prove by absolute, clear, and convincing proof that he has dealt with his sin, developed the requisite godly character, and become a man worthy of emulation in the church. If doubt exists, the church should exercise care. The sinner must demonstrate his restoration to godly character beyond any doubt.

3. Character-building takes time. We are not a patient people. We want instant gratification, instant rewards. The building of Christlike character does not work that way. That is why the Bible refers to Christian leaders as elders. It takes time to develop the character and maturity necessary to become a role model to the Body of Christ.

Why do so many leaders fall into sin today? We base leadership on talent, charisma, and personality – natural abilities – instead of insisting on the development of godly character. It is both odd and sad that many American churches would rather have a young pastor with charisma than an older one with character. That character takes time and when it is shattered it takes even more time to rebuild. Reputation and influence follow the same pattern.

Many churches have "restored" their pastors after a few weeks or months of "healing" after a moral failure. The results are usually not good. When we do not give a man time to rebuild his life and character we are setting him up for more temptation and failure. It is not an act of kindness and affirmation but an inducement to further sin.

I believe that a man can rebuild his character and theoretically become qualified against to be a leader in the church. However, it takes time. He must address his failures, repent genuinely, seek restitution, go to the root of his problems and correct them, and demonstrate a genuine transformation of heart by the power of

Christ. It takes years for that process to happen. Years, not weeks or months.

4. The passage of time alone does not mitigate sin. Just because something is 25 years in the past does not mean that it has been properly dealt with or that the sinner has no remaining responsibility. It requires repentance and a genuine attempt to make restitution for his sins. God's forgiveness is available but people are sometimes less gracious. That man must seek the forgiveness of his injured ex-wife and his children. There may be other relationships broken or damaged by his sin. He must face those and deal with them. An angry ex-wife who spreads tales about the man's past failures can seriously damage his ability to lead. Children who resent their father's past failures may prevent him from being an effective leader. Only when a man has sought God's forgiveness and by his grace seen God bring some level of restoration in these relationships is any kind of leadership position desirable in any way. Much more than the passage of time is required.

5. The decision is for the local church and should be respected. The restored sinner too often acts as if he has a right to demand reinstatement. A man with a truly repentant and submissive heart will not be assertive or demanding toward the church he fellowships with but will submit to that church's authority and policy. No one has the right to demand leadership in a church. It is given by the church to those it chooses; those its people can follow as they grow in Christ. A man who insists on leadership positions is giving indication that he is likely not ready for such a position. Leadership is given in the church, not demanded or taken.

6. Divorce is not a trivial offense! This is commonly argued when one asserts that a divorced and remarried man can be qualified as the husband of one wife in spite of his divorce. We are accused of ignoring the sanctity of marriage and treating divorce as if it is no big deal. That is a specious argument.

If we elect a pastor who was once a drug addict it does not mean we are endorsing drug addiction, does it? If we elect a pastor who once was a criminal, does it encourage a life of crime? No, it says that we believe in the power of the gospel to overcome sin. When we elect a divorcee as a deacon we are not endorsing divorce but praising the God who was able to take a broken man and rebuild him. That is the gospel way. The biblical ideal is not compromised when we accept the reality of broken world exceptions. We glorify the work of God in the lives of sinners when we believe that they can be redeemed for more than a seat on the back row of the church.

Divorce is anything but trivial. It is a serious sin, a variation from the intent of God. But it is not beyond the reach of redemption either and balancing these truths is the key to understanding.

7) The decision depends on the circumstances. I am not saying that divorce is not a factor in qualification or that anyone is eligible to lead no matter the circumstances of his divorce, how often he has been divorced, or how long it has been since the divorce. In most circumstances, I would argue against a man who has been divorced because of his own sin serving in leadership positions in the church. I am arguing here that there may be limited and rare circumstances in which such a man may be able to experience the transforming and renewing power of Christ to such an extent that he might be qualified again to serve as a leader.

The primary marriage qualification is that a man must be "the husband of one wife," or "a one-woman man." He must be faithful and devoted to his wife, demonstrating the kind of godly love and

What the Bible Says about Divorce, Remarriage, and Ministry

leadership toward her that he will be required to show toward the Bride of Christ. All of us in leadership were one unqualified but the work of Christ has made us fit. A man who was once unfit as a husband can be made fit by the work of the Spirit. Godly leadership s about who a man is not what he used to be. I hold out the possibility that a man who failed in marriage by his own fault in the past could repent, make restitution, and demonstrate his renewed character over time to his church, that he has become a one-woman man by Christ's power, qualifying him for leadership in the church. On the other hand, if I am vetting such a person or voting on his candidacy, I am "no" vote unless I am blown away to the contrary. The burden of proof goes against the man who failed. There are several things I would look at.

What was his life situation when he had the failure? Was he an unsaved man who later came to Christ? Was he a church leader who failed his church responsibilities? I would be much less likely to seek restoration of someone who betrayed both his family and the church than someone who was unsaved at the time.

I would want to know about the family he sinned against. Has he sought forgiveness from the ex-wife and children he offended? Is there bitterness and brokenness? If there are negative family issues, these will affect his ability to lead.

What is the position he is seeking? I would be more likely to support such a man as an assistant pastor or a deacon than as an elder or a senior pastor. These are not absolutes, but they are factors. What kind of church is he going to serve? Biblical qualifications don't change but people's expectations do. If the church is a First Baptist, County Seat, in a town of "respectable" (on human terms) people, it may be more difficult. If it is a church in an area where sin has broken lives more visibly, it might be a better fit. Leadership is about the people we lead.

There are many other issues that the church would have to consider as it makes its decision. In the vast majority of cases when a man fails in leadership or when a man has broken his marriage covenant he is better off serving God without the responsibility and visibility of leadership. There may be times when, in the grace and plan of God a guilty part may be restored by God's mighty hand. That man may be able to rebuild his life, his reputation, his integrity, and his leadership ability to the point where some positions are available to him again...theoretically.

It would be the rarest of rare situations in which I would support such a thing.

Chapter 10: Advice to the Divorced

I have received two common responses from this study through the years. The first is from prohibitionists who resist the idea that divorce is not an automatic and permanent disqualification from leadership in the church. The second is from divorced men who have are deeply hurt because they want to serve God and their church has slammed the door in their face because of their marital past. They are frustrated because they sense a call of God on their lives to preach or to teach and are not allowed to practice their gifts. They feel diminished because some churches still treat the divorced as second class citizens in the kingdom of God. And some are still angry, carrying the burden of how unfairly they were treated by a wife who left for another man, a church that sided with the wife, or some other perceived injustice.

I would give these men some advice that goes beyond the basic theological and exegetical truths I have argued in this study. I understand the hurt, the disappointment and the frustration that you go through. I am believe there are some truths that could help you as you try to deal with your emotions, your past, and your desire to serve God.

1. Keep your focus on your biggest job.

It is not your highest priority to find a ministry position, but to become the most Christlike man of God you can possibly become. The key to biblical leadership is character, not position. If you want to be a leader in the church of Jesus Christ, don't focus on gaining a position in the church but make it your goal to meet every one of the qualifications in 1 Timothy 3 and Titus 1. Exhibit the fruit of the Spirit from Galatians 5, not the works of the flesh. Be an encourager not a complainer.

In a previous pastorate, we were selecting deacons. A man came to me with a question. "Dave, is it okay if I nominate myself?" Technically there was nothing in our bylaws that prevented a man from putting himself forward as a deacon, but I knew that two things were true. First of all, I knew that no one else was going to nominate this man. He was not ready to be a deacon. He had holes in his character big enough to drive an Amtrak train through. And I knew that the very fact that he wanted the position so badly was a sign of the fact that he was not qualified for it. His self-promotion was a symptom of everything that made him a poor candidate. At our last deacons' meeting we were having a discussion about the nomination process we were going through. We give our deacon nominees a paper which describes the qualifications from 1 Timothy 3 and asks them to evaluate themselves. Most of the men judge themselves to be unworthy and refuse to serve. It is those men that we want to serve – those who see themselves as unworthy but that the church sees as qualified.

If you have been divorced in the past, people may tend to see you as deficient in some way, and that hurts. They may tend to judge you and wonder what you did that caused your divorce. You may have done everything you can to preserve your marriage. She found another man and you forgave her, but she left anyway. But still people see you in a negative light, and that hurts. There is nothing you can do about that.

But you can be a man of God. Love God with all your heart. Serve him faithfully. Live for him without reserve – abandoned fully to the purposes and plans of God. And let God work in your heart to make you everything he wants you to be. Don't answer accusations and derogations with defensiveness and justifications, answer it with Christlikeness. Let your life answer the accusations and the negative impressions.

2. Clean the slate.

Because of the status of divorced people in the church, they can often become defensive and deflect any blame about the past. I've been married for nearly four decades and I've done quite a bit of counseling with couples. I've yet to see a marital problem that was fully the fault of one side or the other. When we talk about the innocent party, we speak of the person who did not commit adultery or leave the marriage, but no one is sinless.

If you are divorced, you need to face up to whatever failures on your part that contributed to the downfall of the marriage. Your wife left you and you did not deserve that. It was wrong. But would you admit before God that maybe you were not the best husband you could have been? Maybe you did not do all you could to meet her needs and to demonstrate Christlike love? That does not excuse her infidelity – not in any way. But it is not her sin that is your concern right now, it is yours. Stand before God with an open heart and an open Bible and ask him to reveal your failures and flaws. Don't defend yourself but open yourself to the searchlight of God's holiness. Passing the buck and pinning the blame are easy, but looking at your own flaws in the light of God's word and seeking to correct them by God's power is the better way.

Make your focus being a man of God. Pastor? Elder? Deacon? That is secondary. Focus on being Christlike and exhibiting the fruit of the Spirit every day. As you become more like Christ your church will find itself more and desiring to imitate you as you imitate Christ. Be a leader in spiritual things whether they ever elevate you to a position of leadership or not. I believe that God will bless that faithfulness.

3. Let God promote you.

Should you be a deacon? Should you be an elder? Should you be allowed to preach or be considered for a pastoral role? Can we not trust the plan and perfection of God? Do you believe that poor God up in Heaven wants you to be a pastor but he simply cannot get it done because of the pharisaical attitudes of those self-righteous men who stand in the way at your church? He needs your help to get the job done? You have to constantly lobby and complain and work the church to "get what is coming to you."

If you don't know God is bigger than that, your marital history is not the main impediment to your service and leadership in the church. Be the man that God wants you to be and trust God to promote you to the position that he wants you to have. As you read your Bible, note how many powerful men tried to stand in the way of the purposes of God. Did any of them succeed? Of course not. God can either change hearts or move people out of the way. If he has a purpose for your life he will accomplish that and he doesn't need you to lobby for the position you want, scheme to get your way, pressure people to see things as you do, complain about the injustices of life, or work in the power of the flesh to accomplish what you think should happen.

When you trust God, none of that is necessary.

4. Be faithful in the little things.

In a previous ministry we were trying to figure out how to grow our youth ministry and were considering a paid position. A young man who had begun attending our church showed interest in being hired for the position. When we suggested that he work on a volunteer basis to build up the youth ministry while we transitioned into a paid position he showed no interest. If there was no money he was unwilling to do the job. His unwillingness to work in the small things made us wary of trusting him with the responsibility of our youth group.

You want the church to recognize you as a leader, to accept that God has called you to ministry, or to service as a deacon? Serve in any way they will allow. Be faithful in any small way you can. If they will give you a class of seventh grade boys to teach, be the best seventh grade boys teacher that you can be. If they will let you mow the lawn, mow it well. If they ask you to visit the hospital, visit faithfully. Whatever you do, do it for the glory of God and be faithful in whatever you do. Don't sit on the sidelines waiting for the church to recognize your calling and refusing to minister in any way until they do.

5. Don't hide your past.

There is no need for you to tell your sad story to every person you meet, but if you are being considered for a position of leadership in a church, it is essential that you inform them fully of the basics of your marital history. As painful as it might be to be informed that you will not be considered for a position because of a past divorce, it will be even more painful if and when that history is found out in the future (and truth has a way of surfacing) and not only do you have to deal with the past but offer an explanation for your failure to disclose it.

If you are a member of a church, find out what the church's policy is about divorced leadership before you allow your name to be advanced in the nomination process. Don't "go with the flow" and allow the process to proceed hoping no one will ask the tough questions. That is one of the consequences of either your own sin or the sin of your former spouse.

If you are applying for a pastoral position at a church, you need to disclose the past early in the process. I don't have extensive experience in the application process – I've not changed churches often and those have been unique circumstances. My suggestion is that you do not include your divorce on your resume, but that you reveal it in the discussion process with the search committee early in the process. Provide a brief but honest explanation. Realize that in many circumstances this will end the interview process.

There are other options open to you if you are searching for a pastoral role. Most churches have a contact email on their job listing. Make a contact and ask if divorced candidates will be considered. If they say yes, apply and attach an explanation of your circumstances in a separate letter. Or, offer yourself as a supply or interim pastor. Sometimes those relationships can develop.

If you are looking for a role as a pastor, you must face reality. Many churches will not even consider your resume and those that do will likely slip it to the bottom of the pile. Trust God and serve him. If he is in it, he will lead you. But he will not be honored by deception and will not bless it.

6. As a last resort, find a new church.

People are far too quick to leave churches today. You do not leave the church because you have a spat with someone; you work it out. You don't leave a church because you don't get your way; you learn to walk in humility. You don't leave a church because of minor doctrinal differences. But sometimes there are serious differences of philosophy or approach that necessitate a change in churches.

If you are a divorced man who wants to serve God and you attend a church that has a strict policy against divorced men serving in any positions of leadership, you likely only have three options. First, you can attempt to change the minds of the leaders of your church and convince them that divorce should not be an automatic disqualifier from service. That will likely be a difficult road to walk. Prohibitionists are not easy to convince even for someone like me. I have never been divorce. My only reason for advocating what do is my belief that it is the teaching of scripture – no personal axe to grind. You may find those in your church will write off your opinions as self-promotion, a desire to justify your own failure. A second option is to accept your status at that church. Maybe the fellowship and discipleship of a church makes it worth it to continue at that church, putting your desire to lead on the altar and giving it up. The other option is to seek a church that believes what is taught in this book, that the divorced can be restored to leadership positions in time. Those are your options and you can prayerfully consider which way God would direct you.

Just do not be a malcontent. Better to find a sympathetic church than to be a thorn in the flesh at a church with stricter policies. No church is for everyone. If you are constantly negative, politicking, arguing, or lobbying others, it may be best for you to simply find another place to serve. If you cannot submit to the leadership and their policies and serve with joy, it might be best to move on to a place where you can.

A Final Word

I have heard the pain and frustration coming from men whose desire to preach, to serve God and his church have been frustrated by events beyond their control. Your wife decided she did not want to be a pastor's wife and she left. Maybe she found another man and broke your heart. Your ministry dreams came crashing down and no matter what you do, many in the church will not support you.

But I would encourage you to humble yourself before God, learn from your mistakes, and focus on building godly character and becoming more and more a man of God every day. Trust him to promote you in his time to whatever position of responsibility and leadership he has designed for you. Focus on serving the Body of Christ not demanding certain positions in it. Focus on your character more than on being recognized by others. Focus on loving others, not lobbying for what you believe you should have.

Then, whatever happens, you will be a blessing to the church of Jesus Christ and useful servant in the kingdom of God.

Chapter 12: Advice to Churches

Our oldest son became overly attached to his pacifier as a baby. We finally decided he needed to give it up and so we took it away. It was traumatic. He would scream for it when he was put down in his crib for a nap or for bedtime. No one should have to be anyone's first child and we were learning by doing. Taking away his pacifier made him insecure and fearful. Even as adults we are like that. We love security and stability. Churches tend to love the security of absolute rules and policies. Do this all the time. Never do that. Many churches have attempted to establish such universal policies to govern the selection of leaders. Can a pastor, an elder, or a deacon be divorced, or be married to someone who is divorced? Yes. No. Many churches want to give a universal answer. It is soothing and simple. But there is no such simplicity warranted in Scripture. It is not my intent to call anyone a baby, but only to point out that as churches we often revert to universal policies to avoid wading through difficult scenarios on a case-by-case solution. Life in a sinful, broken world is never that simple and we cannot comfort ourselves with such fixed policies if we wish to be biblical.

Imagine that we are selecting deacons in our church and a few men have been nominated. The first is a man who just a couple of years ago left his wife for another woman. He is repentant and loves the Lord, but he also admits that the destruction of his first marriage is his own fault. Another man was married young, right out of high school. Things did not work out and they went their separate ways. There were no children and he has lost touch with her. In his loneliness after the divorce, he started attending church and found the Lord. He met a godly young woman, also a young divorcee. They have been married now for over 25 years, have raised a family in the church, three children who serve the Lord faithfully. They are an example to everyone of a devoted, godly marriage. There is another man who has been nominated. He was in leadership about ten years ago, but his wife fell in love with her boss, a wealthy man, and ran off with him to make a new life. He was heartbroken and tried to reconcile with her, begging her to return. Against his wishes the divorce came through. He is still single, raising his two children, who rarely see their wayward mother. Another man, though saved, got caught up on the fast track to success. He was making money hand over fist, while ignoring both his family and his faith. His wife walked out with the kids. This woke him up and though he tried, she refused to believe his changes were genuine. She remarried her high school sweetheart and after a few years he too remarried. It's been five years now, and they are happy. He is still working hard and doing well, but his priorities are different now and everyone can see it.

Which of these men is qualified to serve? No blanket policy is possible here and it is absurd to treat them all as if they are the same. A church must look at each of these men, study their lives, and determine if they can lead and serve in the body of Christ effectively. Surely a man who was divorced before he was saved and has demonstrated a 25-year godly marriage ought to be treated differently than a man who left his wife two years ago for another woman, even if he has truly repented. Should a man whose wife left him for someone else years ago be treated as if he committed a disqualifying sin? It is understandable that a church would want to establish a simple and universal policy that would govern every circumstance? Yes, it is understandable, but not possible. Life isn't like that in a fallen world. All divorces are not created equal and cannot be treated as equal.

As with the Pirates Code, which was "more like guidelines than actual rules," we must look for biblical guidelines, not absolute and easy rules, that will help churches make these tough decisions. You cannot make a blanket policy and be biblical at the same time. The Scriptures have a foundational principle (lifelong covenant), two exceptions (adultery and abandonment), and an abuse of authority clause to protect women. And applying those in real-life situations is difficult. So, here are some helpful principles to remember.

Guidelines for Churches

1. The church must balance two competing concepts in dealing with marriage issues.

This is not just true with divorce and remarriage issues, but with many other issues as well. God is holy and God is love. His holiness demands that he punish sin and the wages of sin is death. He also demands, among the redeemed, that we "be holy, as I am holy." Since God is a righteous, holy, pure, and sinless God we who have been redeemed must live in holiness and seek to walk in righteousness by the power of the indwelling Spirit. When it comes to marriage, this holiness demands that we hold fast to the original intent, the cornerstone of marriage. "One man, one woman, pure before marriage, faithful after marriage, till death do us part." We must stand unreservedly, unapologetically, and uncompromisingly on the side of marriage as a lifelong covenant between a man and a woman. We must seek to build strong marriages and help struggling couples stay together and find the joy God intended. We can never give in to the worldly mindset of "cut your losses and move on." We always seek to stand on the side of "till death do us part" marriage.

On the other hand, we live in a broken world, a fact that even God recognized according to Jesus. Because of sin, God led Moses to make allowances. Jesus established the divorce exception, then Paul added the abandonment exception and the abuse escape. In this sinful world, our duty is to seek to understand and apply the redemptive power of Christ. My dad used to say (with some frustration, I think), "If you ever find a perfect church, don't join it. You will just mess it up." We are all sinners, every single one of us. Jesus paid for our sins at the cross and the church must always be agents of his amazing grace.

Keeping these two competing passions balanced is always difficult. When we emphasize grace, it can often come across as though we do not care about the divine standard of righteousness. When we emphasize holy standards, it can sound harsh and condemning to those who have violated that standard. Keeping the balance is a constant juggling act.

When I was a youth pastor, I tried to teach often on the importance of sexual purity through the teen years. Later, I talked to a young person who had been molested and this person told me that every time I taught about purity, they had the thought, "well, it's too late for me." I felt horrible. In holding up the standard of sexual holiness I sometimes failed to communicate God's grace (and the fact that if someone is molested, he or she has been sinned against and has not committed sin – but that is another subject for another book). It is a constant balance.

We must keep that principle of lifelong covenant marriage, the cornerstone of the biblical revelation, front and center in all that we teach. It may be old-fashioned and be a message disdained in our culture and even sometimes devalued in the church, but it is God's unchanging bedrock for society. This is not something the church can surrender on and survive. We must hold this truth. It is not homosexuals or liberals or anyone else who is the greatest threat to marriage, but Christians who fail to live out the dictates of our faith, who fail to honor the sanctity of marriage day by day in the way we love our spouses or raise our children. And godly marriages that build godly homes can among our greatest testimonies to the world of the reality of Christ and the power of the word of God. When they see the original intent of God lived out in us and through us, it is a marvelous testimony.

The world must also see grace at work in us. It is not enough for the church to simply condemn homosexuality; we must also love homosexuals and seek to reach them in Christ's love. That is a constant tension in the so-called marriage wars. How do we love people who live in willful contradiction to God's word?

Too long, divorced people have felt as if they were second class citizens of the kingdom of God. That is simply not acceptable. A redeemed and forgiven sinner is a redeemed and forgiven sinner, whether that sin is lust, pride, greed, or divorce. And in the church we have often treated divorce as a sin that is beyond the redemptive work of God.

A few years ago, on the way back from a high school reunion, I drove across the Rio Grande Gorge Bridge near Taos, New Mexico. Which would be better, do you think, to drive off that bridge to the right or to the left? I got out and walked the sidewalks on both sides and I am qualified to state unequivocally that driving off to either side would be a horrible mistake. The only safe thing is to stay in your lane as you drive across the bridge. That is what the church must do. It must stay in the center, balance love and holiness, standards and forgiveness. Yes, we must uphold the truth of God's word, that marriage is a lifelong covenant, but we must also be agents of God's forgiveness and grace, his restoration, transformation, and renewing power. To drive off on either side will have devastating consequences.

2. The Church must uphold the gospel as it deals with divorce.

Let us tread carefully here, because a charge of denying the gospel is the most serious one can make. Prohibitionists who disagree with this book's position love Jesus and love the gospel of Christ's saving grace. However, the implications of the strict prohibition view run counter to the thrust of the gospel. No one is intentionally denying the work of Christ, but the effect is problematic nonetheless.

Do we believe 2 Corinthians 5:17? "If anyone is in Christ he is a new creation; the old has gone, the new has come." When a man comes to Christ, he is made a new person in Christ. The Christian gospel is about hell-deserving sinners being forgiven and transformed. What message do we send when we exclude a man from leadership because of something that happened prior to his conversion to Christ? What message do we send when we act as if divorce is a sin without a statute of limitations, as if the blood can never cleanse and never rebuild?

"What kind of testimony do we give if our pastor is divorced?" Many are worried about the public testimony of the church if it allows leaders who are divorced. It is a valid concern; the church

What the Bible Says about Divorce, Remarriage, and Ministry should not lower the standards of holiness and ought to be concerned about the witness and reputation it maintains. However, Paul, cataloging sins, said, "such were some of you." The church is not a country club for those who have never been touched by failure, but a hospital where sinners find healing. When a man whose life was broken but restored by Jesus Christ stands to testify of the grace and power of Jesus, that is a wonderful testimony. That is the gospel. That is power of Christ.

The way that we deal with divorce must not only testify the cleansing power of the blood of Christ, but to the rebuilding and transformational power of Christ. Christ does not cleanse us from sin and then set us on the sidelines forever. When a city is devastated by a disaster the people rebuild. When a believer is devastated by sin, the Holy Spirit rebuilds.

May we never treat divorce as if it is a sin beyond either the cleansing or transformational power of Christ. Of course, we must remember that not all divorce is sin, but even when sin is involved it is not beyond the reach of God's grace.

3. Do not treat divorce as a special category of sin.

The church has done precisely that. We treat divorce differently than any other sin a person could commit. Imagine that a man commits a murder – cold-blooded and cruel – but he gets off on a technicality, then gets saved. He will go around the country sharing his testimony and churches will rejoice about how Christ saved a brutal murderer. Church leadership is open to murderers. Drug dealers? There are plenty of redeemed and reformed drug dealers in pulpits all over America and many serve as elders and deacons as well. We glory in the transformational power of Christ to take a drug dealer, save him, and make him a man of God. A church leader who is a former drug dealer? No problem. What about someone who

141

practiced premarital sex? Are you kidding? I would guess that men like me, who were virgins when we got married and have had sex with only one woman all our lives are in the minority – even among pastors, elders and deacons in evangelical churches. I have heard pastors give testimonies about their promiscuity before they were saved, or before they got their lives focused on the Lord, and the church amens those testimonies. You name it, church leaders have done it.

Divorce stands alone. A man can have premarital sex and be a pastor but cannot be divorced and be a pastor. Can someone explain that? A pastor can be an ex-con, but not a divorcee? Please flesh out the logic of that.

We have put divorce into a special category of sin. Think about this. Until just recently, my denomination's mission board had a hard and fast rule against divorced people serving as missionaries. Imagine this scenario (based on actual events in previous churches I've served). Two young men grow up in the same church. One is walking with Christ and marries a young woman in the church, thinking she loves Jesus too. Turns out her faith is not real and she abandons him for another man. He is devastated, but eventually, after a few years, finds a godly Christian woman. Another man "sows his wild oats" and lives an immoral life, even fathers a couple of children out of wedlock. He never marries their mothers though. Later, God gets hold of his life and he gets married. Both men now serve the Lord. The irony is that the young man who served God and married young was not eligible to be a missionary, but the young man who practiced premarital sex and fathered children out of wedlock is, because he didn't marry the women he slept with. That kind of hypocrisy is often the result of blanket rules and strict prohibitionist views.

Divorce must not be put in a separate category. A result of sin, it may or may not be sinful itself. If adultery, abandonment, or abuse has occurred, God himself has set exceptions in this broken world and permitted divorce. Treating divorce as universal, unpardonable sin is not upholding biblical standards but violating them.

4. Each man's qualifications must be separately, carefully, and prayerfully reviewed.

We cannot chew on the pacifier of universal policies. The church must look at each situation individually and decide if a man is qualified to lead. There are certain factors that must be considered.

What were the circumstances of the divorce? Did the man abandon his wife and his children for another woman? Was he unfaithful? Did he seek the divorce? Or was he the "innocent party?" Did his wife leave him for another man? Was he abandoned? It is crucial that we ask the tough questions. If a man does not want to answer those questions, it would be an indication he may not be ready for leadership in the body of Christ. The church has to get the story on the divorce. It matters.

How long ago was the divorce? If a man is currently going through a divorce, no matter how innocent he is, he's not ready to lead. He needs to work on home and family. He needs to heal. If the divorce was 25 years ago and he has demonstrated godly character to the church for over 2 decades, should the divorce be an impediment? Time is a significant issue.

Has he demonstrated to the church that he is a man of character, a "husband of one wife" today? Every one of the qualities listed in 1 Timothy 3 and Titus 1 are present tense character qualities. The question is not, "Do you meet this character quality and have you always met this quality?" No one has always met these qualities. That is the purpose of Christian growth, of sanctification. The question is whether a man, today, is a "one-woman man" and has an exemplary reputation in the church and community. Has he made mistakes in the past? We all have. We are not born, or even born-again, ready to lead. It is a process of growth. I have always been faithful to my wife, but I have grown in understanding how to be a good husband and how to meet her needs. I'm a better "one-woman man" today than I was 30 years ago.

Does the church respect him enough to follow him? That is the quintessential question for leadership. Paul told people that they should "follow me as I follow Christ." Leaders in a church must be able to say, "Follow me to Christ." I remember a deacon in my first pastorate. He had been divorced in his youth, long, long ago. But by the time I knew him his children were adults and he'd been a faithful husband and father for a quarter of a century. He was respected in that church. He was a man who loved God and loved his family. He was a deacon, a servant of the church, qualified biblically and qualified by the respect of the church.

A church must weigh all of these questions. It would be nice to have a simple check list, but doesn't work that way. We must weigh this factor and that, gather the evidence as a church, and make a decision. Fortunately, we have God's word to guide us and the Spirit to lead us. These kinds of decisions are never easy but that is how it must be done.

5. Does time negate even a guilty party's sin?

This is a thorny issue. A man who divorces and remarries without biblical warrant is sinning against God. But God forgives sin and restores lives. If a man repents of that sin and works through the years to rebuild his character and his reputation, can he at some point be restored to leadership in the church of Jesus Christ? A murderer can be forgiven, and in time become a leader in a church. All pastors, all elders, all deacons share the fact that they are forgiven sinners. We all have a past. So, the question is this. Can a man who was the guilty party in a divorce ever be restored to leadership in the church? Does time heal that wound?

We discussed the healing and rebuilding power of the gospel. Does not the cleansing power of Christ and the transforming power of our Savior require that we at least ask the question if a man who cheated on his wife and ruined his marriage can have a significant leadership position in a church at a future time?

Undeniably, unquestionably, and without reservation, we must say that the church must forgive sinners, regardless of the sin. A fallen pastor, a cheating church leader, they must be granted forgiveness and the restoration of fellowship. The church that rejects fellowship with a sinning leader who repents has sinned against Christ. Forgiveness is essential, not an option.

But forgiveness and restoration to leadership are two different things. If I failed in my marriage, my church should receive my repentance and restore my membership, but that does not mean that the pulpit would be my home anymore. Someone else would sit in the big chair.

Here is the key issue. Jesus said that a man who remarried a woman when there had been no adultery was committing adultery with her. What did he mean? Did he mean that such a marriage would continue to be a sinful relationship, that it would be, in essence, ongoing adultery for the rest of their lives? Or was he simply referring to the initiation of the marriage? I do not know anyone who counsels such couples to divorce a second time, but is the second relationship a constant offense against God that disqualifies the man from leadership positions?

Because of Jesus' words, I believe that is a serious question. If a man is the innocent party, there is no support for exclusion. This is a more difficult question. If a man committed such a sin prior to conversion, I would not consider it an automatic disqualifier from service. On the other hand, a pastor or other church leader who sullied his office, shamed his church and besmirched the name of Christ is probably best not to seek such a position again. I cannot see myself sitting under the preaching of such a man, even after many years.

If a man is truly repentant, has demonstrated that over time, has rebuilt a godly life and demonstrated that to the church, there ought to be avenues of service and ministry open to such a man. However, we must not ignore the words of Christ or do anything that would cheapen the sanctity of marriage. I do not agree with those who believe that moral failure is a permanent disqualification from leadership, but it is a significant disqualification.

6. Do not jump the gun on restoration.

The forgiveness of Christ is immediate and it is complete. When I repent my sins are fully washed away, the stain is gone and God remembers them no more. But that does not mean that the consequences are gone or that a man should be fully restored to his position of leadership should be restored immediately, or even quickly.

We have seen high profile cases where a leader failed and then took a couple of weeks off for "restoration." Nonsense. Leadership is based on character. It takes time to build character. When a leader fails it is evidence of a serious character defect. How many times have you seen someone apologize for a failure and say, "that just wasn't me." Yes, it was. You did it. It was a character flaw that caused you to make that choice and you need to rebuild your character before you can become the leader you need to be. That takes time.

Only a foolhardy church restores a sinning leader in a week, or a month. The process of restoration takes years. If a man is the innocent party of a divorce, he ought to pull back from leadership for a time. A man who was in sin should take even longer. Make sure that character is rebuilt to handle the responsibility of leadership or the sin will simply be repeated.

7. Moral failure leaves a limp.

David was restored and forgiven, and he continued as king of Israel (yes, I'm aware that king of Israel and pastor of a local church are two different roles – boy, am I aware of that!). But David walked with a limp ever after. He lost some of his moral standing with his family, his ability to lead them. Not only did the baby conceived in sin die as a result of his sin, but there was devastation that seemed to follow his family thereafter. From 2 Samuel 12, which records David's sin, to the end of the book, there is one tragedy after another for this man after God's own heart. While I believe that pastors who sin can be restored, and that divorced men can be excellent deacons, elders and even pastors, our sin can leave consequences in our lives that cause us to walk with a limp. It is always better to not sin than to sin and be restored. Always!

A Final Word

No church can ignore this topic anymore. The divorced are among us and in many churches are now the majority of adults. We can no longer afford to simply do what we have always done or deal with this topic based on our traditions. We must take seriously the nuanced teaching of Scripture, holding up both the sanctity of marriage and the grace of our Lord to those whose lives have been broken by sin – theirs or others.

May the grace of God protect our marriages and build our churches.

Simple Summary Statements on a Complex Topic

1. Marriage was created by God as a lifelong covenant between one man and one woman.

2. Because our sin broke this world, God made exceptions to the lifelong marriage principle in the case of adultery and abandonment. He also gave an escape for women whose husbands abuse their authority, permitting them to separate and live single lives instead of living under their husbands' abusive authority.

3. Leadership in the church is based on godly character developed over time and demonstrated to the church, allowing the leader to be an example to the church of Christlikeness. One of the required character qualities is to be the "husband of one wife."

4. A "husband of one wife" is a man, married to one woman, who loves her as Christ loved the church and faithfully serves her in a way that serves as a role model to the church and demonstrates his ability to serve well the Bride of Christ.

5. Leaders in the church are redeemed sinners whose processed of transformation has proceeded to the point where they can lead others in their transformation. No leader is sinless.

6. Divorce is never the intent of God, but it is not always sin. When a divorce takes place under the exceptions established in Scripture, it is regrettable but it is not sinful.

7. Those who have been divorced are not automatically disqualified from service in God's church. If the divorce took place on biblical grounds, it was ended in God's eyes and he was free to remarry. Such divorces do not disqualify a man from service as a pastor, an elder, or a deacon.

Books by Dave Miller

Significant Servants: Ordinary People, Eternal Work

An examination of a Five-Step process revealed in Scriptures that explains how ordinary people made significant contributions to the Kingdom of God.

Brick Walls Picket Fences: Balancing Doctrine and Unity

How can the church balance its desires to know God's word and have sound doctrine with its desire to walk in unity with other believers? Dave Miller lays out four levels of biblical truth with an appropriate unity response for each.

Disqualified? What does the Bible Say about Divorce, Remarriage, and Ministry?

Does the Bible actually say that the divorced are eliminated from leadership positions in the church? Dave Miller examines the biblical evidence and posits a "redemptive view" which emphasizes the renewing and restoring power of the Cross of Christ.

Disqualified?

Printed in Great Britain
by Amazon

78298041R00097